The NEGRO IN THE CARIBBEAN

By

DR. ERIC WILLIAMS

B.A., D.Phil. (Oxon.)
Assistant Professor of Social and Political Science
Howard University

Former Prime Minister of
Trinidad & Tobago

EWORLD INC.

Buffalo, New York
14209
eeworldinc@yahoo.com

COVER DESIGN: *EWorld Inc.*

LETTERING: *INDUSTRIAL FONTS & GRAFIXS*

COVER PHOTO: *18TH CENTURY DRESS:AGOSTINO BRUNIAS 1770-1796*

ISBN 978-1-61759-008-5

Formally published by
A&B Publishers Group
Brooklyn, New York
ISBN 1-881316-68-8

Published by

EWORLD INC.

Buffalo, New York
14209
eeworldinc@yahoo.com

12 13 14   5 4 3 2 1

EDITORIAL FOREWORD

To give the layman a panoramic but not superficial over-view of the Caribbean area, its islands and their people, is in itself a large service. But this study goes further to set the West Indies meaningfully in the perspective of their historic past, as well as to present the problems of the present in a challenging and constructive interpretation looking toward their future. At a time when the Caribbean has become one of the crucial foci of national, hemispheric and international politics, such an approach, and the more comprehensive understanding it makes possible, seem imperative.

Dr. Eric Williams, the young Negro author, has peculiar competence to carry all these converging interests through to integrated interpretation. Born 1911 in Trinidad, graduate of Queen's Royal College there in 1931, he studied on an Island Scholarship at Oxford, 1932–1939. There he won his B.A., with Double First in the Honour School of Modern History, and then proceeded to his D.Phil. degree with a thesis on *The Economic Aspect of the Abolition of the British West Indian Slave Trade and Slavery*. In 1940 he revisited the West Indies on a Rosenwald Fellowship, gathering material for this study, and two prospective more comprehensive works on *The Sugar Economy of the Caribbean* and *Capitalism and Slavery*. As now for several years a teacher in the United States and a citizen of the Americas in the larger sense, he is eminently fitted to link up hitherto isolated segments of the racial problems common to this hemisphere.

From the racial angle, it is hoped that this study will furnish a closer and sounder bond of understanding between the Negro-American and his brother West-Indian, known all too limitedly merely as a migrant rather than with regard either to his home background or with reference to our common racial history and problems. From the national angle, shared too by the Negro minority, it may also be expected to contribute to a more realistic inter-American understanding and to suggest ways of helpful economic, political and cultural collaboration. Both selfishly and altruistically, for national as well as international interests, it behooves the United States to pursue constructive economic and political policies in the Caribbean, and without a realistic and objective understanding of the situation and its problems such an enlightened, long-range program is impossible. The issues of this analysis present a challenge to us which, rightly solved, will lead to the constructive enlargement of Western democracy.   *Alain Locke.*

CONTENTS

THE NEGRO IN THE CARIBBEAN

Foreword and Acknowledgments

CHAPTER	PAGE
I. The Islands	1
II. The Slavery Background	11
III. The Economic Structure	17
IV. The Condition of the Negro Wage-Earner	32
V. The Land Problem and the Negro Peasant	46
VI. The Middle Class and the Racial Problem	57
VII. Native Education	70
VIII. The Political Problem	83
IX. The Future of the Caribbean	99
Reference Notes	110
Bibliography	115
Conspectus Table: Statistics of the Caribbean	118

ACKNOWLEDGMENTS

To three of my colleagues at Howard University, I am indebted for careful reading and constructive criticism of this manuscript;—Dr. W. O. Brown of the department of Sociology, experienced student of the race question in South Africa, Puerto Rico and elsewhere; Professor Ralph J. Bunche of the Department of Political Science, now Senior Researcher in colonial affairs of the Office of Defense Information, and Dr. Alain Locke, Professor of Philosophy and Editor of this series. Their kind and valuable suggestions have been very helpful and have removed many, though not all of its defects.

The Editor, after commissioning the study over two years ago, has generously allowed me to get acclimated to this country, and readily consented to further postponement so that I might re-visit the islands for more recent observation and materials. That visit, and this study in its present form, was only made possible by the generous grant of a Fellowship from the Julius Rosenwald Fund, which permitted me to spend the summer of 1940 in Cuba, Haiti, the Dominican Republic and Puerto Rico. In this way I was able not only to check, from first-hand sources and observations, my own personal knowledge of the British Caribbean, but to make contacts in the French and Spanish areas which were as pleasant as they were instructive.

Eric Williams.

Howard University,
January 30, 1942.

THE NEGRO IN THE CARIBBEAN

CHAPTER I

THE CARIBBEAN SCENE:

"THE ISLANDS"

Stretching from the Gulf of Mexico to the Atlantic Ocean is a wide expanse of sea dotted with a number of islands called, after their original Indian inhabitants, the Caribbean Sea and the Caribbean Islands. In the West, Cuba is within easy reach of Florida; to the South and East lies Trinidad, at the mouth of the Amazon, within a day's sail of the Venezuelan coast. Lying in between are a heterogeneous collection of islands, varying in size but uniform in climate and economic structure, while far to the North, well in the Atlantic, stands Bermuda in its isolation. On the South American continent are the Guianas, the El Dorado of Sir Walter Raleigh, vast stretches of territory shared between England, France and Holland. These, with British Honduras in Central America, represent, apart from Canada, the only European areas in the Western Hemisphere. For reasons of convenience they may well be considered together with the Caribbean islands to which they are similar in economy as well as in the racial character of their population.

Discovered by Columbus in his search for a westerly passage to India, the name he gave them, "West Indies", is still in vogue today. Originally the mon-

1

opoly of the Crown of Spain, imperialist rivalries up
to 1900 transferred various islands to other powers.
The British West Indies are a collection of nineteen
scattered island units. Martinique and Guadeloupe
remain as survivals of a magnificent French empire in
the Western Hemisphere which once included Canada,
Louisiana and Haiti. The Dutch are still represented
by Curacao and its dependencies. Spain and Denmark
have vanished from the scene, the one driven out, the
other bought out by the United States. Cuba, Haiti
and the Dominican Republic have succeeded in maintaining a precarious independence which they wrested
from Spain and France.

In area the islands proper comprise some 90,000
square miles, somewhat more than one-third the size
of Texas, with a population of over thirteen millions,
or more than double that of Texas. By far the largest island is Cuba; the size of Pennsylvania, its population is approximately one-half. The Dominican Republic, double the size of Vermont, has a population
four times the population of that state. Haiti, its
population three times that of Nevada, is one-tenth
of the area of Nevada. The British West Indies
comprise an area somewhat more than one-third of the
area of Indiana with a population approximately one-
third less. In the French islands of Martinique and
Guadeloupe, a population more than double that of
Delaware lives in an area less than half the size. The
Dutch colonies, one-seventh the size of Delaware, have
a population less than that of Wilmington. American
Puerto Rico, one-twelfth the area of Pennsylvania,
supports the population of Philadelphia.

The islands vary in size from the 44,000 square
miles of Cuba to the 166 of Barbados and the 32 of
Montserrat. The population of Cuba is over four
millions. Puerto Rico, one-twelfth the size of Cuba,

2

has a population slightly under half that of its larger sister. The 166 square miles of Barbados support a population of 193,000. The density of population is enormous, the struggle for survival consequently fierce. Every acre of cultivable ground in Barbados is in use; the density of population is 1163 to the square mile, and is even higher, if only cultivable land is taken into consideration. Puerto Rico supports an average of 506 persons per square mile, or 1375 for each square mile under cultivation. The estimated density per square mile for Trinidad is 229, for Tobago 241, for Grenada 665, for Guadeloupe 442. Much of Cuba is too mountainous for cultivation; of Haiti's 10,700 square miles, only one-quarter is plain, the rest is mountainous land.

At first sight the mainland areas present a different picture. The three Guianas, in area larger than California, have a total population less than that of Los Angeles. British Guiana, larger than Minnesota, has a smaller population than Minneapolis. French Guiana, larger than Maine, can boast of a population, convicts included, only six per cent of Maine's. British Honduras, larger than Massachusetts, has only half the population of Cambridge. The density of population in British Honduras is six per square mile. In British Guiana it is less than four. But less than 200 of its 90,000 square miles are under cultivation, giving a working density of nearly 1700 per square mile. These islands and colonies need living space far more than the totalitarian countries with their much-vaunted claims.

The climate of the entire area is in the main tropical. It is, however, more equable than tropical. The annual mean temperature is about 80 degrees for all the islands. The temperature too is uniform all the year round; the average temperature for the warmest month seldom exceeds 82 degrees, while the size of the islands leaves them exposed to the sea breezes, and the humidity of the summer months in the United States is unknown. The frequent assertion that white men were unable to stand the strain of manual labor in the islands is in fact a myth. White settlers were deliberately encouraged by the Spanish Government to settle in Cuba and Puerto Rico, and the Cuban tobacco industry has always been, in comparison with its counterpart in Virginia, a white and free industry. The Dutch islands of Saba and St. Martin are the home of pure white north Europeans who have lived there as peasant workers for several hundred years, and one day Hitler may remember a pure German colony of peasants in Seaford, Jamaica, descendants of immigrants in 1834. Moreover, the climate of Cuba and Haiti is rather sub-tropical than tropical, hence perhaps one reason why the mortality of the Negro slaves in these islands exceeded the mortality in other areas in the Caribbean. A few miles outside of Port-au-Prince in Haiti is the summer resort of Kenskoff. At sunset one would think one was in Switzerland rather than in the tropics. There are only two seasons, the wet and the dry—the one very wet, the other very dry. The wet season is the season of the hurricanes, those tremendous storms which Edmund Burke once described as a correction of the planters' vices or a humbler of their pride. The period of hurricanes is indicated by an old rhyme:

June, too soon.
July, stand by.
August, come it must.
September, remember.
October, all over.

They come up suddenly, leaving a trail of havoc behind when the sun returns shining bright, like the ebullient inhabitants of the islands, quick to lose tempers,

4

cause great damage, and then re-emerge smiling as if nothing had happened. A severe hurricane in 1928 caused property losses estimated in Puerto Rico at fifty million dollars; another of 1932 the loss of 225 lives, the injury of 4,800 persons and property damage estimated at thirty million dollars. Most of the islands are of volcanic origin. The volcanoes are practically all extinct, though the people of the Caribbean have not forgotten the year 1902. In that year Mont Pélé in Martinique erupted. In forty-five seconds the capital, St. Pierre, with its 28,000 inhabitants, was completely wiped out; the ashes covered the northern half of St. Vincent, causing the loss of some 2,000 lives. A wreck of a steamer crawled into the harbor of St. Lucia. "Who are you," shouted the watching crowd, "and where do you come from?" "We come from hell," was the reply. "You can cable the world that St. Pierre no longer exists."

In this climate tropical products are in their natural element. Sugar cane, coffee, cocoa, cotton, tobacco, coconuts; tropical fruits such as pineapples, bananas, oranges, grapefruit, avocado pears, plums of all sorts, grow in abundance and, as it were, naturally, together with a variety of others whose names would hardly be known outside of the Caribbean,—the guava, mango, sapodilla, balata, soursop and sugar-apple.

Tropical vegetables are legion, making the table of the well-to-do colored bourgeois a treat for the most fastidious gourmand—eddoes, dasheen, yams, cassava, cush-cush, plantains, calaloo, okra and a host of others. The luxuriant vegetation of the tropics is everywhere; the greenheart (whose hard, heavy wood is eminently suited for docks, quays and piles), the mora, mahogany, cedar, purpleheart, and, the best known of all, the stately palm. Flowering trees and shrubs in profusion add that charm and scent which have made the

5

beauty of the islands almost legendary: the immortelle with its flame-colored flowers, that serves as a shade for cocoa plantations, and which the Spaniards call "cocoa-mother", the jasmine, bougainvillea, hibiscus and poinsetta. Spices abound, cloves, nutmegs, peppers, tonca beans. Birds of exquisite beauty, some peculiar like the humming bird; fish of all sorts, some delicious like the kingfish, red fish, flying fish, others dangerous like the shark, the barracouta, the stingaree; poisonous reptiles, such as the rattlesnake, the coral snake, the mapipire and boa constrictor; alligators, scorpions, centipedes, lizards, turtles, tortoises, all contribute to the diversity if not security of the landscape. There are fine beaches everywhere—Silver Sands and Bathsheba in Barbados, Doctor's Cave in Jamaica, Grand Anse in Grenada, Varadero in Cuba. The Kaieteur Falls in British Guiana are the highest in the world and would make six Niagaras; smaller ones are found elsewhere. The natural harbors, the blue skies and clear water make these islands the resort of tourists in large numbers. What Charles Kingsley wrote of one island is true of all: "The island, from peak to shore, is like a gorgeous jewel, hanging between the blue sea and the white surf below, and the blue sky and white clouds above." Nature in the Caribbean has been as kind as man has been unkind.

Everywhere, in every island, is seen the pre-eminent product, mile upon mile of sugar cane, unvarying, monotonous, signifying the magnificent wealth of its owners at one pole and the magnificent misery of its cultivators at the other.

It is ironical to recall today that it was tobacco and not sugar which at the beginning was the gift of the New World to the Old. The sugar cane was brought from the Old World to the New; though the New World was, as it were, called into existence to supply

6

sugar to the Old. But if sugar still retains today pride of place among the islands' products in the world's markets, it is by no means the only product for which they are famous. The bananas of Jamaica and Martinique have a well-deserved reputation in the markets of England and France. Sufficient on a cigar is the word "Havana". The "Blue Mountain" Coffee of Jamaica fetches the highest price in the world coffee market. The bay rum of the Virgin Islands is as celebrated for external use as is the rum of Jamaica for internal use. The name Curacao connoted to the world only a justly famous liqueur before the Nazi threat to the Western Hemisphere revealed that it was also an island in the Caribbean. Trinidad is the largest producer of oil in the British Empire. In addition, Trinidad possesses in the Pitch Lake one of the natural wonders of the world. Cuba has mineral deposits, small in quantity, but valuable as strategic war materials. The Guianas have deposits of gold, diamonds and bauxite, indispensable in the construction of aeroplanes.

The great age of the Caribbean, however, was the seventeenth and eighteenth centuries, when sugar occupied in the international market the place later usurped by cotton and taken today by oil and steel. Today the islands would have remained in relative oblivion except for curious tourists and romancers and treasure hunters: Hitler saved them from that hardly undeserved oblivion. For the Caribbean is one of the most important seas, strategically speaking, in the world. It lies athwart the trade routes from the Atlantic to the Pacific. Who commands the Caribbean commands the Panama Canal. Kingston, Jamaica, is 550 miles from that vital artery; Trinidad, 1170; Barbados, 1225; St. Thomas, 1035; Curacao, 696. Bermuda is less than 700 miles from New York, and San Juan, Puerto

Rico, 1400. Nassau, capital of the Bahamas, is less than 1200 miles from Miami; Trinidad is 3122 miles from Rio de Janeiro, and Barbados 2000 from Pernambuco. Bermuda is 2800 miles from the Azores, and 2700 from Dakar.

The Caribbean islands are, in fact, a vital link in the chain of hemisphere defence. The Caribbean has become for the United States "our sea", the "American Mediterranean", with Puerto Rico as its Gibraltar. That fact has been brought home to the American public, by press and radio. The United States Government has acquired leases on bases in the British islands; the Pan-American Conference held at Havana in July, 1940 was summoned to discuss the future of the European dependencies in the Caribbean should the European war result in a victory for Germany. The United States is keeping a sharp watch on Martinique, with its large stock of gold, its aeroplanes and its capital ships, and above all its harbor, Fort-de-France, incomparably the best between Cuba and South America. A recent agreement with the Dutch Government makes the United States partly responsible for the defence of Dutch Guiana, dangerously close to Dakar.

An island, however, is more than a naval or aerial base; it is home for many thousands who teem on it as ants on an anthill. It is a scene not only of military activity; it is the stage for the struggle for survival of people living in dire poverty. In these poverty-stricken areas the overwhelming proportion of the population is Negro or mulatto. Pure Negroes are estimated at over 90 per cent in Haiti, 77 per cent in Jamaica, 74 per cent in the British Windward Islands. The Dominican Republic is overwhelmingly mulatto, about 68 per cent of the population being of mixed blood, while a further 18 per cent is pure Negro. In Haiti, where

8

they constitute the ruling class, the mulattoes are less than 10 per cent of the population; in Jamaica 18; in the British Leeward Islands 17. Negroes and mulattoes make up between 80 and 90 per cent of the population of the Dutch islands. The percentage of Negroes or people of Negroid descent in the former Spanish colonies is smaller, partly because of the policy already referred to of encouraging white settlers, partly because of the great losses suffered by the Negroes in the Cuban wars of independence against Spain. But a distinguished authority in Puerto Rico estimates the colored element at somewhere between 30 and 50 per cent, whilst in Cuba it can confidently be reckoned as at least one-third. Conversely, whites are more numerous in these former Spanish colonies, which were home and not exile to the settlers from Spain. Among the other colonies, the percentage of whites is highest in Barbados, where they constitute seven per cent of the population. Nowhere else in the area is the proportion nearly so high. A few Chinese are to be found in places, as well as some Jews; Indians, introduced after emancipation from British India, and Javanese from the Dutch East Indies, constitute about one-third of the population of Trinidad, two-fifths of British Guiana and almost half the population of Dutch Guiana.

So large a Negro population must necessarily be an object of interest to the Negro minority of the United States. If the traffic between the two Negro groups has been one-way in the past, from islands to the North American mainland, the future will surely see a greater movement in the other direction, from the United States to the islands. These islands are also of great interest to the student. For studies of African survivals, of relationships between a variety of races,— Negro, whites of all nationalities, Chinese, Indian— the islands are a great unexploited laboratory. The political scientist will find in Bermuda one of the oldest assemblies in the world, after the House of Commons; he will see in twentieth century Barbados an Elizabethan survival in the form of the vestry system. But particularly today these islands and their inhabitants must be of great interest to the American public in general, now that the Pan-American policy demands closer cooperation and a mutual understanding of one's neighbors. Strategic considerations must not be allowed to overshadow the human element of the equation. It is this human element, basically Negro, that this study mainly proposes to treat.

CHAPTER II

THE SLAVERY BACKGROUND

The original inhabitants of the Caribbean islands were speedily exterminated by the Spanish conquerors, of whom it has been said that first they fell on their knees and then they fell on the aborigines. The islands were useless to their owners without a labor supply. It was to satisfy the labor requirements of the West Indian islands that the greatest migration in recorded history took place. This was the Negro slave trade.

The slave trade introduced the African Negro to the Caribbean stage. This great inhumanity of man to man had its origin not in contempt for the blacks or in any belief that the black man was destined for slavery. These were the later rationalizations invented to justify what was in its origin basically an economic question, one which can be expressed in one word—Sugar.

The establishment of the sugar industry created the demand for labor in the West Indian islands. That demand was for a constant supply of cheap labor, black, brown or white, with the emphasis on the cheapness of the labor rather than the color of the laborer. It happened that in the fifteenth and sixteenth centuries the cheapest labor was black labor. The Spanish planters discovered that one Negro was worth four Indians; the British planters, in their turn, realized that the money it would take to buy the services of a white indentured servant for ten years would buy a Negro for life. There was, in fact, in the Caribbean not only black slavery, but white and brown as well. But neither the white nor the brown men were forthcoming in sufficient quantities to supply the demand; Africa had inexhaustible human resources. The white indentured servant, too, was rewarded, after the expiry of his contract, with a small grant of land. These new freemen were too poor and their land too insignificant to afford the vast outlay of capital required for establishing a sugar plantation. The white indentured servants, too few to become a regular labor supply, were, therefore, a nuisance. The transported Negro, on the other hand, in a strange environment, handicapped by his ignorance of the white man's language, was pre-eminently fitted for continuous exploitation as he could be kept completely divorced from the land.

This, then, was the origin of the Negro slave trade and Negro slavery. It was a choice, from the sugar planter's point of view, of Negro labor or no labor at all. Sugar meant slavery; only incidentally, and by process of elimination, did it come to mean Negro slavery. Thus was the Negro introduced into his new habitat, and drawn into the orbit of Western civilization to make his contributions to that civilization. If today he is the white man's problem, he was in the sixteenth and seventeenth centuries the only solution of that problem.

The Western World is in danger of forgetting today what the Negro has contributed to Western civilization. The American continent would have had to pay a high price for the luxury of remaining a white man's country. No sugar, no Negroes; but, equally true, no Negroes, no sugar. "Someone had to pick the cotton." That was not why "darkies" were born; but it was certainly to cultivate the sugar cane and later pick the cotton that they were transported from Africa.

It was, in fact, sugar which raised these insignificant tropical islands from the status of pirates' nests to the dignity of the most precious colonies known to the

12

Western World up to the nineteenth century. It was the Negro, without whom the islands would have remained uncultivated and might as well have been at the bottom of the sea, who made these islands into the prizes of war and diplomacy, coveted by the statesmen of all nations. These black "bundles", these "logs", as the Negroes were referred to, meant sugar together with other tropical products. Between 1640 and 1667, when sugar was introduced, the wealth of Barbados increased forty times. All the European wars between 1660 and 1815 were fought for the possession of these valuable Caribbean islands and for the privilege of supplying the "tons" of labor needed by the sugar plantations. Between 1760 and 1813 St. Lucia changed hands seven times.

Tremendous wealth was produced from an unstable economy based on a single crop, which combined the vices of feudalism and capitalism with the virtues of neither. Liverpool in England, Nantes in France, Rhode Island in America, prospered on the slave trade. London and Bristol, Bordeaux and Marseilles, Cadiz and Seville, Lisbon and New England, all waxed fat on the profits of the trade in the tropical produce raised by the Negro slave. Capitalism in England, France, Holland and colonial America received a double stimulus—from the manufacture of goods needed to exchange for slaves, woolen and cotton goods, copper and brass vessels, and the firearms, handcuffs, chains and torture instruments indispensable on the slave ship and on the slave plantation; and from the manufacture of colonial raw materials,—sugar, cotton, molasses. The tiniest British sugar island was considered more valuable than the thirteen mainland colonies combined. French Guadeloupe, with a population today of a mere 300,000, was once deemed more precious than Canada, and the Dutch cheerfully surrendered what is today

13

New York State for a strip of the Guiana territory. These islands were the glittering gems in every imperial diadem, and Barbados, Jamaica, Saint Domingue (to-day Haiti), and then Cuba were, in that order of succession, magic names which meant national prosperity and individual wealth. The wealth of the sugar barons became proverbial. Signs abounded in England and France, the "West Indians" held the highest offices and built magnificent mansions, which in Cuba, with a due sense of their importance, they called palaces. Sugar was king; without his Negro slave his kingdom would have been a desert.

This contribution of the Negro has failed to receive adequate recognition. It is more than ever necessary to remember it today. England and France, Holland, Spain and Denmark, not to mention the United States, Brazil and other parts of South America, all are indebted to Negro labor. As Mr. Winston Churchill declared four years ago: "Our possession of the West Indies, like that of India, . . . gave us the strength, the support, but especially the capital, the wealth, at a time when no other European nation possessed such a reserve, which enabled us to come through the great struggles of the Napoleonic Wars, the keen competition of commerce in the 18th and 19th centuries, and enabled us not only to acquire this appendage of possessions which we have, but also to lay the foundations of that commercial and financial leadership which, when the world was young, when everything outside Europe was undeveloped, enabled us to make our great position in the world."

Slavery was fundamentally the same everywhere, but it is important to notice a significant difference in the cultural pattern. As a necessary instrument of production, the Negro's condition did not vary whether his owner was Latin or Anglo-Saxon. But where the Anglo-Saxons had plantation colonies, with only the

14

bare minimum of white owners, agents, supernumer-
aries and slave drivers, the Spanish colonies were home
to the white immigrants, and the slaves benefited ac-
cordingly. As soon as the Spanish colonies, however,
began to produce for the world market, Spanish slavery lost its patriarchal character. This happened in
Cuba but not in Puerto Rico, and in Cuba relatively
late as compared with the British and French colonies.
Hence, possibly, the absence of the extreme racial tension characteristic of French St. Domingue and the
Southern States. The Anglo-Saxon, too, was apprehensive that baptism, requiring instruction in the English tongue, would give the Negroes a common language and thereby foment sedition and revolts. The
Latin, on the other hand, insisted on baptism and
Christianity for his slave. Laugh at the Pope's sanc-
tion of slavery or his Catholic Majesty's prosecution
of the slave trade; the cultural pattern presents a dis-
tinction of great significance. Spanish laws, and French
to a lesser degree, were notoriously milder to the
slave, and it is a sad commentary on the nature of
early democracy that the Negro slaves were treated
most harshly in the British self-governing colonies.
When Trinidad, for instance, passed into British from
Spanish hands, the British Government refused to abro-
gate the Spanish laws and to concede self-government
to the planters. Popular franchises in the hands of
slaveowners were the worst instruments of tyranny
ever forged for the oppression of mankind. The greater
percentage of whites, too, in the Spanish islands
reduced the disproportion between the races which was
characteristic of the British colonies, and which, after
Saint Domingue had gone up in the flames of the slave
revolution, made all whites in the Caribbean fearful of
slave conspiracies. It is perhaps in this fact that we are
to find a partial explanation of the comparative absence
of racial tension today in the former Spanish colonies.

Kind treatment and Christianity might mitigate slavery, they alone would not abolish it. If the Negro slave eventually became, at various times in the nineteenth century, a free man, the reason is to be found not only in the belated recognition of morality and Christian precepts but also in the fact that slavery, as an economic institution, had ceased to be profitable. That is why slavery in the British islands was abolished fifteen years earlier than in the French and fifty years earlier than in the Spanish islands. Emancipation of the Negro was a juridical, a social and political change. In the eyes of the law the slave, formerly the property of his master, a human beast of burden completely in the power and at the discretion of his owner, became free, with all the rights, privileges and perquisites pertaining thereto. But emancipation was not an economic change. It left the new freeman as much dependent on and at the mercy of his king sugar as he had been as a slave. It meant for him not the land, which was incompatible with the requirements of the capitalist sugar industry, but the Bible, which was not at variance with that industry. It meant a change from chattel slavery to peonage, or, as has been said in another connection, a change from the discipline of the cartwhip to the discipline of starvation. The slave was raised to the dubious dignity of a landless wage laborer, paid at the rate of twenty-five cents a day in the British islands. Sweet are the uses of emancipation! To free the Negro it was necessary not so much to destroy slavery, which was the consequence of sugar, as to alter the method of production in the sugar industry itself. This simple point is essential to an understanding of the situation of the Negro population in the Caribbean today. The black man, emancipated from above by legislation or from below by revolution, remains today the slave of sugar.

16

CHAPTER III

THE ECONOMIC STRUCTURE

The abolition of slavery, in those islands where the land was already appropriated, left the Negro with no alternative but to continue his former occupation. In the absence of mineral resources, except in Trinidad, Cuba and the Guianas, agriculture continues to be the main industry. The Trinidad oil industry employs 14,400 persons and asphalt 650, as compared with 23,800 in the sugar industry. British Guiana's mining industries, bauxite, gold, diamonds, provided employment for less than 3000 people in 1938. An exception to the rule is the Dutch West Indian colonies, whose import and export trade centers around petroleum. They are conveniently located for the oil of Venezuela and Colombia, which is brought by pipe lines to the huge refineries on the islands. Elsewhere agriculture predominates. Roughly half of the occupied population in the British colonies is engaged in agriculture; more than half of all the workers, and two-thirds of the male workers, of Puerto Rico are directly engaged in agriculture. A mere seven per cent of the Haitian population is urban. In addition, the sugar mills, refineries, rum distilleries and tobacco factories, are directly dependent on agriculture. Fluctuations in prices in the world markets, the devastation of hurricanes, competition from more favored areas, all react on the large majority of the population, and consequently affect, to a greater or smaller degree, the Negro population which finds in the agricultural labor to which it has been accustomed since the regime of slavery, its main occupation and chief sustenance.

In this agricultural picture pride of place goes to the sugar industry. Exports of sugar and by-products represent 95 per cent of the total exports of Barbados and 97 per cent of Antigua. In St. Kitts-Nevis and Cuba the proportion is about four-fifths; in the Dominican Republic the average for the decade 1929–1938 was nearly two-thirds. Sugar has always constituted more than half of the total exports of Puerto Rico under American control; in 1938 it was over three-fifths. British Guiana and Guadeloupe are dependent on sugar and its by-products for three-fifths of their exports; sugar accounts for half of the exports of the American Virgin Islands, 45 per cent of St. Lucia's. Even in areas that are more diversified than is normal for the Caribbean, sugar plays no mean role. In banana-land, Jamaica, sugar represents one-fifth of the exports; in the land of coffee, Haiti, sugar exports increased from less than three per cent of total exports on an average of the years 1916–1926 to 14 per cent in 1938–1939 and nearly one-fifth in 1939–1940. Haiti was once the sugar bowl of the Antilles; it was also the greatest slave mart. Sugar is king in the Caribbean as much as it ever was during the regime of slavery.

Two-thirds of the cultivated land in Martinique and one-half in Guadeloupe are devoted to sugar. Half of the cultivated area in Barbados is planted to cane, two-thirds in St. Kitts, one-third ·in British Guiana, one-sixth in Jamaica, one-tenth in Trinidad, four-fifths in Antigua. The entire population of St. Kitts and Antigua is dependent upon sugar, two-thirds of the population of Barbados, one-half of British Guiana, one-third of Trinidad, one-tenth of Jamaica. In Puerto Rico nearly half of the working population is employed in sugar; whereas 100 acres in sugar employ an average of forty-six persons, the same acreage in other cultivation employs an average of thirty-one persons. Sugar is the most important source of purchasing power in the island; without sugar the budget cannot exist. Sugar pays thirty million dollars a year in wages, 40 per cent of the total wages paid to all agricultural laborers. The Negro in the Caribbean is at the mercy of an agricultural autocrat whose rise and fall in the world market has little effect on the picture of unrelieved misery which sugar has always produced in the islands.

The sugar industry is still the source of great wealth. An indication of this wealth is the enormous influx of American capital since the war of 1898 which drove out Spain. It has been estimated that ten millions of American money are directly invested in Haiti, forty-one millions in the Dominican Republic (three-fourths of this in agriculture), six hundred and sixty-six millions in Cuban enterprises—about one-quarter of all such American investments in the twenty Latin American Republics. More than one-third of this investment is in sugar, though the money value of this sugar investment declined from five hundred and forty-four million dollars in 1929 to two hundred and forty in 1936.[1] Thirty million dollars are invested in the Puerto Rico sugar industry alone; sugar accounts for 90 per cent of the investments in the Dominican Republic, 54 per cent in Haiti. Uncle Sam is the "Sugar Daddy" of the Caribbean.

American companies in Cuba control three-fifths of the acreage in cane, nearly three-fifths of the workers in the sugar industry, and more than one-third of the active sugar factories.[2] Up to 1914 Haiti had stringent laws governing the ownership of land by aliens. The old order is being imperceptibly restored. American corporations are increasing, in number, size and influence. The Haitian Agricultural Corporation and the Haitian American Development Company—both

19

sugar corporations—control respectively 1415 and 10,868 acres. A third company, Standard Fruit, owns 2500 acres. A decision of the Supreme Court of Puerto Rico handed down in 1935 describes the situation in that island: "the census of 1935 shows that 251,000 acres, or one-fifth of the agricultural land, is employed in the production of sugar cane: that no less than 196,757 acres, or a little less than 70 per cent of the total area planted to sugar, is the property of, or is controlled almost exclusively by, absentee shareholders (in continental United States); that the companies thus organized and controlled normally manufacture 59 per cent of the total of sugar produced by the island, thus controlling almost 40 per cent of the agricultural wealth of the island." From 1901 to 1934 the area planted to sugar cane in Puerto Rico increased about four times, production eleven times. The quantity of sugar exported by Haiti increased eight times between 1916 and 1939. Yield per acre has been increased enormously; modern methods have made production immeasurably more efficient.

The number one crop in the area has been a very paying proposition. The average profit in the British sugar islands is six per cent; the sugar firm of Tate and Lyle, with a capital of forty million dollars, made a profit of forty-five million dollars in five years, and in 1939 declared a dividend of $13\frac{1}{2}$ per cent on ordinary capital. Four American companies dominate the sugar industry of Puerto Rico; in 1936 they earned over eight and a half million dollars. The South Porto Rico Company paid over a period of thirty years a steady dividend of eight per cent on preferred stock; in 1920 it paid 120 per cent, the Fajardo Sugar Company over 100.

Sugar, clearly, is a valuable crop. The enormous dividends of absentee shareholders who never see the islands provide the background for a consideration of the remuneration paid to those who produce the wealth. The abolition of slavery in the British West Indies was followed by incessant demands from the planters for labor from India, and between 1842 and 1917 a never-ending stream of indentured laborers flowed to the British sugar colonies, chiefly Trinidad and Guiana, to meet the labor requirements and compete with the "lazy" Negro. Between 1833 and 1917, when the system was abolished, Trinidad received 145,000 Indians, British Guiana 238,000. Up to recent times, the demand for labor by Cuban sugar plantations dominated by American capitalists was responsible for a large-scale introduction of black laborers from Haiti and Jamaica until in exasperation, the native Cuban workers, black and white, well organized and opposed to the "africanization" of the island, forced the government to suppress this indentured traffic and repatriate the aliens. Between 1913 and 1924 Cuba obtained 217,000 laborers from Haiti, Jamaica and Puerto Rico; in the single year 1920, as many as 63,000 from Haiti and Jamaica. According to the 1931 census there were nearly 80,000 Haitians resident in Cuba. Of these 30,000 were repatriated between 1936 and 1937. The average annual exodus from Jamaica, largely to Cuba, was 10,000 for the half century before 1935; in the five years ending in 1935 approximately 31,000 were repatriated, chiefly from Cuba. The Dominican Republic dealt more drastically with the imported laborers; a wholesale slaughter of Haitians took place in 1937. The official estimate of those massacred is 5000, though unofficial estimates are much higher. A further 5000 were repatriated, but in 1937 there were still 60,000 Haitians resident in the Dominican Republic, which has since insisted that 70 per cent of all employees must be Dominicans. Sugar cultivation is still a question of labor; indentured labor, once white, then yellow or brown, is now black. What a Trinidadian Mayor said in 1888 is true of indentured labor all over the Caribbean and planter attitude to it: "no men could be more grandiloquent about their intention, in all they proposed to do, being the development of the resources of the island; no men could be more determined, as shown by their measures, to do no other thing than bolster up the more or less nominal owners of sugar plantations."[3]

"An industry", stated the Colonial Secretary (white) of Trinidad in 1937, "has no right to pay dividends at all until it pays a fair wage to labour and gives the labourer decent conditions." A Barbados Commission in the same year repeated the warning: "We have been impressed by the high dividends earned by many trading concerns in the island and the comfortable salaries and bonuses paid to the higher grades of employees in business and agriculture. If the whole community were prosperous and enjoyed a comfortable standard of living, high dividends might be defensible, but when these are only possible on the basis of low wages the time has clearly come for a reconsideration of the fundamental conditions and organization of industry. . . . A fundamental change in the division of earnings between the employer and his employees is essential if hatred and bitterness are to be removed from the minds of the majority of employees."[4] The male laborer in the British West Indies gets an average of 25 cents a day, with a lower wage for women. The average earnings of male laborers on sugar-cane plantations in Puerto Rico in 1933 were $3.50 per week, for a 23-hour week. A recent study has been made by the School of Tropical Medicine in Puerto Rico of conditions on a sugar-cane plantation purchased by the Puerto Rico Reconstruction Administration and manned

22

predominantly by Negro labor. This study gives an average annual income for farm laborers of less than $120 per worker.[5] The minimum wage of a field laborer in the Cuban sugar industry is 80 cents a day. A social and economic study of the West Indian islands, says a South African professor, is necessarily a study of poverty. In the words of the Puerto Rico Reconstruction Administration: "the sugar industry does not satisfy the requirements of the economic life of the island and should be adjusted in order to meet the needs of the people."[6]

It must not be assumed that the sugar industry, while it is the greatest offender, is the only offender. Wages are equally low in other occupations, with the difference that the capital required in coffee, fruit, and tobacco cultivation being less than that required in the sugar industry, the percentage of alien ownership is reduced, the number of small proprietors greater. A study of nearly 6,000 families with over 34,000 members in various coffee, fruit and tobacco regions in Puerto Rico reveals a mean daily wage rate for all areas of 60 cents and an annual income per worker of less than $100 for three-fifths of the farm laborers investigated, while the remaining two-fifths earned less than $150.[7] The average daily wage for unskilled labor on the oilfields of Trinidad is 72 cents, while oil companies declared dividends of 45 and 30 per cent, and while the profits for 1935–1936 were four times the wages bill.[8] In a recent broadcast speech the Secretary of State for the Colonies in England attributed the poverty of the British West Indies to their lack of "highly prized products". This is absurd. There is great wealth produced in the West Indies; but it follows its absentee ownership abroad, and only a little stays behind.

In the urban areas of the Caribbean the Negro wage-

23

earner is scarcely better off. The Cuban Census of 1907 shows a predominance of the following occupations: carpenters, domestics, laundresses, tailors. Add to these the police force—wholly black or colored in all the areas—bus conductors, railwaymen, and one exhausts the openings available to Negroes. In the skilled trades they are clearly better off than as domestics or in the laundry business. But no one could speak of the urban areas as a paradise for the Negro wage-earner.

Proof of this is to be found in the needlework industry of Puerto Rico. The Puerto Rican woman, white or Negro, had inherited from the Spanish regime a tradition of high quality needlework; the "runaway sweatshop operator from New York or New Jersey" was not slow to discover the possibilities. Mass production has meant not only a transfer of Puerto Rican handicraft from Fifth Avenue to smaller concerns; it has meant wholesale export of the raw material to Puerto Rico there to take advantage of the plentiful labor and low wages. Today these textiles constitute one-sixth of Puerto Rico's exports and provide an annual income of seven to ten million dollars in the form of wages and commissions. Normally valued at twenty million dollars, the industry provides work for 65,000 persons in factories and home. Essentially it is a sweatshop industry. According to the United States Department of Labor, earnings in the factories in 1934 averaged $12\frac{1}{2}$ cents per hour, while 90 per cent of the home workers earned less than four cents an hour. The attempt of the Federal Government to enforce a 30-cent-an-hour minimum resulted in a virtual shutdown of the industry. The inference is clear: sweated industry or no industry. This quotation on low wages from a bulletin of the Agricultural Station of the University of Puerto Rico may be taken as indicative of the attitude of the official class as a whole over the area: "With laborers who produce less, it is impossible to pay the same salaries as in the Mainland. The lofty aims of the hours and wages legislation are appreciated, but it is considered that a blanket application of a wage minimum to areas so dissimilar in the labor productivity per man can only place the area of lower productivity per man at a disadvantage."[9] Always the same theme, with variations, always the same old refrain—"it does not pay", despite the high dividends. We may ask, in exasperation, as the Royal Commission to the British West Indies asked in 1897: "Sugar does not pay—this and that does not pay. Is there anything that does pay anywhere?" Like the peasant in feudal France, the Negro laborer in the Caribbean pays for all.

The plight of the Negro wage-earner is aggravated by the intermittent character of employment available. In sugar cultivation there is a long "dead" season between harvest time, which represented, in slavery days, a great drain on the planter's resources. The modern absentee corporation is not as shackled by obligations to its "free" labor force as was even the slaveowner to his slaves. Total unemployment is by no means negligible even in the busy season. This is what expert investigators say of a study of certain coffee, fruit and tobacco regions in Puerto Rico: "The families affected by unemployment are nearly one-eighth of the total number of families investigated and the persons unemployed are about one-tenth of the total number of gainful workers in the surveyed area. In judging the situation it should be kept in mind that this unemployment occurs among P.R.R.A. workers' families and precisely during the months in which the employment rate was highest."[10] In Jamaica in 1935 at least 11 per cent of the wage-earning population were continuously un-

25

employed, and it is the considered opinion of the Labour Adviser sent out in 1938 from England to report on labor conditions in the British islands that "the present prospect (in Kingston) is of a body of some thousands of permanently unemployed maintained by heavy expenditure on what are really relief works."[11] In 1935 nearly half the wage-earning population of Jamaica obtained only intermittent employment, and the government and private employers have deliberately adopted the policy of rotational employment, whereby a man works for two weeks and then is discharged to make way for another—a new version of the theory of the greatest happiness of the greatest number. In Grenada some employers provide five days' work per week, others no more than two. The average for the whole British West Indian area is about three days per week. Laborers in sugar-cane planting in Puerto Rico work on an average thirty-four weeks in the year, only 10 per cent of the unskilled and 41 per cent of the skilled workers being employed during the whole year.[12] The 25-cent-a-day wage in the British islands, the 60-cent-a-day wage in Puerto Rico must be viewed in the light of this under-employment. In the words of a Puerto Rican scholar, Dr. Rafael Picó, "the sugar plantation economy, based on the seasonal employment of thousands of inadequately paid *peones,* does not offer any hope for the amelioration of social and economic conditions; rather it aims to perpetuate the present deplorable situation."[13]

The despotism of King Sugar, in the islands, is perpetuating another unhealthy feature of the slavery regime—a fatal dependence on monoculture, a fatal concentration on a single crop. Monoculture is the curse not of nature but of man. The economy of these islands was always artificial. Producing in the main valuable export crops, they always depended on foreign

26

sources for food imports, and the use of land for the growing of foodstuffs or for pasturage was and is begrudged. It was not altogether the planter's fault. In 1698 the merchants of England sent a petition to Parliament protesting against a law which prohibited the export of corn, meal, flour, bread, biscuit to the West Indies. The law would encourage the planters to grow food instead of sugar, and would thus be detrimental to the home country. Since emancipation sugar has extended its sway and ousted other crops which tended to diversify production and consequently to reduce the dangers of an adverse year. Cotton and coffee very early disappeared from the list of important exports in the British islands. The American acquisition of Puerto Rico has reversed the relative importance of coffee and sugar under Spanish and American rule; it has reduced coffee exports from 20 per cent in 1901 to one per cent in 1938, while tobacco exports too have shown a decline. In 1902 sugar constituted nearly half of Cuba's exports, tobacco nearly two-fifths, minor crops one-eighth. In 1939 the figures were four-fifths sugar, one-tenth tobacco, one-eleventh minor crops. Where the absolute monarchy of sugar has been destroyed, it has been replaced not by the liberal democracy of a diversified economy but by another crop dictatorship. Thus cocoa was for many years synonymous with Trinidad; the banana is to Jamaica in the twentieth century what sugar cane was in the nineteenth. It represents three-fifths of the island's exports and about one-fifth of total world production, and employs two-fifths of the laborers in the island. Limes monopolized the attention of planters, large and small, in Dominica, until the appearance of a fungus disease; coffee represented nearly three-fourths of Haiti's exports on an average of the decade 1916–1926 and one-half in 1938.

27

The persistence of a trend towards monoculture has made the islands more dependent on imported food and reduced the acreage of land formerly devoted to food crops within the various units. Three times as much land is devoted to sugar in Martinique as to food crops. In Puerto Rico, food crops decreased from two-fifths of the total cultivated land in 1899 to one-third in 1929, though the population increased by three-fifths in the same period. Puerto Rico imports all of its fats and oils, all of its wheat, nearly all of its rice and potatoes, nine-tenths of its fish, three-fifths of its pork and legumes. It spends two million dollars a year on peas and beans; one-fourth of its imports in 1940 was accounted for by foodstuffs.

Imports of food are responsible for one-seventh of Haiti's imports, one-fourth of Jamaica's. Despite the diversification program begun in Cuba under the stimulus of the world depression, foodstuffs still constituted more than one-fourth of imports in 1932–1933 as compared with more than one-third for the period 1924–1928. Tinned milk and butter figure largely in the imports, owing to deficiency of cattle. In islands around which fish of all varieties abounds, vast quantities of salted fish are annually imported, while, to make the situation more fantastic, two island dependencies of Jamaica exist largely on the export of salt to Canada for the curing of the imported article. Jamaica spent over a million dollars on imported fish in 1936. In a population of nearly two million in Puerto Rico, only 600 professionals derive a regular livelihood from fishing; the annual catch is barely worth $200,000. In densely populated areas like Barbados, or Puerto Rico, not even if all the land were devoted to food crops could the total population be fed. But that cannot justify the tinned pineapples or tinned soups which one sees in every Puerto Rican grocery store, or the tinned beef and fruit which pass for luxuries in Trinidad. The argument advanced, in Puerto Rico and elsewhere, is that the gross income per acre of land in sugar makes it possible to buy more units of imported food than can be raised on an acre of land in any island. Export crops, it is held, generally yield higher incomes per acre than most of the food crops produced for the local market. Higher incomes, yes; but not to the Negro, forced to work for wages on sugar cane plantations and buy imported food at high prices. What if the price of sugar falls in the world market as the price of Cuban sugar fell from twenty-three to two cents in a few weeks after the last war? The price of food may not fall likewise. What if a World War reduces the volume of shipping and, by increasing insurance costs, increases the already high price of the imported article?

It takes a crisis of the first magnitude to bring home to the rulers of the islands what is clear to the meanest intelligence. The crisis over, back go the planters to the old vice. The Bourbons of the Caribbean, they learn nothing and forget nothing. As far back as 1813 the governor of Demerara* wrote that the colony could raise corn and rice and rear cattle sufficient to supply all the islands, but, he confessed pathetically, "unfortunately these humble paths to certain profit are overlooked by people whose whole attention is absorbed in the expectation of obtaining rapid fortunes by the growth of sugar, coffee or cotton". These humble paths, not so much to profit as to stability, attract attention only in a period of storm and stress. At other times, adequate subsistence for the working population, the social stability which comes from a diversified economy, have meant no more to foreign capital than to the man in the moon.

---

* Now a part of the colony of British Guiana.

The European war has cut off many of the islands' products from their normal markets. In 1934–1935, 99 per cent of Haiti's coffee went to European markets. Decline set in with the denunciation by France in 1936 of the commercial convention with Haiti, but in 1938–1939 Haiti was still dependent on Europe for three-fifths of its coffee exports. Belgium, Holland, Norway and Denmark consumed nearly one-fifth of Haiti's total exports before Hitler's conquest; in 1938–1939, over one-fifth of Haiti's exports went to France. The Dominican Republic found in the United Kingdom a market for three-quarters of its sugar in 1935 and one-half in 1937. The percentage of Jamaican bananas exported to the United Kingdom rose from 16 to 78 in the eleven years before 1935. The British Government, owing to the war, has had to purchase some seven million dollars worth of Jamaica bananas, largely to be destroyed, and even this represents decline of one-seventh in Jamaica's exports. The French islands have been brought to the verge of famine by the British blockade which cut off their trade with the parent country.

In this critical state of affairs a new policy is being developed in the islands, and publicized with all the furore of a great discovery. Puerto Rican officials have suddenly recalled the major food crisis occasioned by a five-week dock strike in 1938. They are now full of wise saws and ancient instances about the need of crop diversity and development of subsistence farms. Haiti's new president places great hopes on rubber cultivation. The Dominican Republic has recently been granted a large loan by the Export-Import Bank of the United States to develop a meat industry which will supply crowded Puerto Rico. "New problems for the British West Indies", say writers suddenly aware of these islands. The problem is as old as the islands themselves, under European control. Years ago an acute observer wrote as follows: "in the multiplicity of evidence that every day brought forth, it became more and more clear that any conclusions that could be drawn would be in the nature of well-established truisms. The observer of whatever kind, and whether he remains in the West Indies for a few weeks or for some years, will find no new panacea for the troubles of these colonies."[14]

Apologists for monoculture—and there are many— argue that the path of wisdom is to concentrate on "the increase of the total volume of agricultural production". This ignores the vital fact that such an increase has already taken place. An exchange economy is no doubt, on paper, other things being equal, superior to a strict self-sufficiency. But in the Caribbean other things are not equal; the Negro, that is the laboring class, loses both ways if it is impossible for him to insist that decent wages and decent living conditions come before dividends in an export crop dominated by absentee interests. Under the present arrangement the Caribbean islands are richly endowed by nature, with a pauperised and impoverished population.

> Ill fares the land to hastening ills a prey,
> Where wealth accumulates, and men decay.

CHAPTER IV

THE CONDITION OF THE NEGRO
WAGE-EARNER

The Negro in the Caribbean, we emphasise, is primarily an agricultural laborer, working for pitifully low wages. As the saying goes, he produces what he does not eat, and eats what he does not produce. He produces sugar, but it is for the world market, and he cannot live by sugar alone. He cannot even afford the refined article and has to be content with brown sugar. His food, as stated above, is largely imported. How much does he eat? The Negro cannot be adequately fed on a 25-cent-a-day wage for three days of the week. The weekly budget of the Barbadian laborer is less than two dollars; of this food costs him seven cents a day.[1] A special study of a small Puerto Rican town reveals a daily expenditure for a family of six of twenty-three cents on food.[2] The price of food is increased by colonial dependence on nations with tariff walls. The Negro cannot possibly buy in the cheapest market; he must buy in the market of his "mother country", and "mother" demands adequate remuneration. The cost added by the Puerto Rican tariff was three-fourths in the case of rice, two-fifths for wheat flour, over three-fourths for dried beans, over one-fourth for codfish.[3]

Evidence of malnutrition abounds over the whole area. A medical visitor from the Dutch East Indies to Trinidad in 1935 was "shocked by the evidence of malnutrition."[4] The laborer in Barbados is fed worse than a gaolbird; he cannot afford milk in his tea; say the planters, he does not like milk![5] The Puerto Rican

32

rural laborer has an income of twelve cents a day for all necessities of life—four cents more than the cost of feeding a hog in the United States.[6] Between two-thirds of the income in the sugar regions and four-fifths in the coffee, fruit and tobacco districts are spent on food: "a sure indication", says one study, "of the inadequacy of an income of which such a high proportion has to be devoted to mere subsistence."[7] Most rural families are heavily in debt; the larger part of these debts is incurred wholly or partially for food. The extent of petty larceny in Trinidad and elsewhere is enormous. It increases like the death rate, in direct ratio to depression and poverty. It represents in the main thefts of food; the only remedy suggested is the cat-o'-nine tails.

Malnutrition means not merely insufficient food, it means defective food. The actual diet of the Caribbean Negro consists of quantity rather than quality, with an undue proportion of carbohydrates and conspicuous absence of fats and proteins. The British West Indian would be at home with the "national" diet of rice and red beans of the Dominican Republic or Puerto Rico. "Most of the people", we read of Puerto Rican sugar conditions, "have only black coffee or coffee with milk for breakfast, codfish and vegetables for lunch and rice and beans for dinner."[8] A study of 884 rural families in Haiti reveals that 15 per cent eat only one meal a day, 45 per cent eat two meals, while of those who eat three times a day, lunch consists of a modest piece of cassava or boiled banana. Over 10 per cent have only black coffee for breakfast, eggs were eaten in the morning by only eight families, at the evening meal by only seven. Some families go two or three months without meat, others spend between two and four cents a week on fish, fresh or dried. A Haitian soldier gets fifteen cents a day for food, prisoners ten cents, inmates of public charitable institutions six to eight cents.[9] A commission of the Foreign Policy Association sent to investigate the problems of Cuba in 1935 estimated the cost of the food needed by a Cuban adult male at $38,[10] a figure far too high for the income of the majority of laborers.

The daily consumption of fresh milk in Jamaica's capital, with its 30,000 children of school age, is one-fifteenth quart per head; the Jamaica politicians say that the Negro prefers condensed milk. The average monthly consumption of fresh meat per head of population in Kingston, Jamaica, is barely one pound, and even this does not represent the true position, for the eaters of fresh beef are almost entirely confined to the middle and upper classes.[11] "The diet of the average worker can be classed at the best only as a maintenance diet, and . . . there is no reason to doubt that many households live on the borderland of extreme poverty."[12]

The results of this deficient diet are devastating. Measurements of 15,500 Puerto Rican laborers, 16 per cent of them colored, reveal that they are shorter and lighter than American army recruits or American adults.[13] The Caribbean islands are distinguished by an enormously high incidence of preventable diseases, many of them traceable directly to malnutrition. Malaria, hookworm, tuberculosis, venereal diseases, wreak havoc with the Negro population. There was a time when the islands were the white man's grave; yellow fever killed them like flies. Health conditions may have improved in the islands, but the official picture of conditions in Trinidad describes every adult above the age of 20 years as affected by deficiency diseases, and the working life of the population reduced by at least one-half. "A condition of lethargy pervaded the whole community, which was only broken on festive occasions or in times of disorder."[14]

34

The major curse of the area is hookworm. Hookworm is essentially a problem firstly of nutrition, secondly, of sanitation. The larva of the hookworm lives in excrement. In dry places, its life is forty-eight hours, in wet anything up to three weeks. Inadequate food renders the Negro peculiarly susceptible to this disease which is produced by defecation in the fields, and is commonest around exposed and insanitary latrines. The larva enters through the pores of the feet. The barefooted Negro therefore has no protection against this disease. Latrines are located far from the place of work, too far for an emergency; many of the filthy dwellings in which the Negroes live are not provided with latrines, or at best with communal latrines, cesspits, the stench of which is unbearable. Of the families investigated in Puerto Rico on a sugar-cane plantation, over two-fifths have no sanitary conveniences of any kind in their homes. In the coffee, fruit and tobacco regions, the percentage is over one-half. "The surroundings of the workers' houses are, in most instances, very unclean, and the latrines are so poorly kept that it is not surprising that many people avoid their use and use the sugar-cane fields and the bushes, thus defeating the primary objective of a privy, which is to prevent soil pollution and the consequent spread of diseases of the gastro-intestinal tract."[15]

Two things, above all, will remedy this situation. Firstly a sewage policy for the islands. A British oil aristocrat, sitting in the House of Lords, has already asked complacently whether Trinidad is "the only place where there are bad houses, no roads, no water, no sewage?"[16] The second remedy is shoes for the population. The Dutch Government eradicated hookworm among the whites of St. Martin by installing a policeman to compel the villagers to wear shoes. It would need an army to compel employers to pay decent wages, if hookworm is to be eradicated among the

Negroes. The Negro cannot buy shoes when he earns 25 cents a day. As the investigators on the Lafayette sugar plantation observed: "three-fourths of the children from 1–4 years of age, three-fifths of the children from 5–9 years and nearly one-half of the children 10–14 years do not wear shoes. In no group do all people wear shoes, the percentage in all ages above 15 years fluctuating from 60 per cent to 69 per cent, except in the age group 65 years and over in which the percentage of people wearing shoes is only 55.7. Another point of interest is that the percentage of colored people wearing shoes is consistently lower than the percentage of white people."[17] All God's chillun may have shoes, but not in the Caribbean.

The ravages of hookworm are eloquently shown in the vital statistics. The percentage of hookworm infection in rural districts of Trinidad varies from 79 to 98, is 69 per cent in certain areas of Barbados and 83 per cent in Puerto Rico. Hookworm, say the British Commissioners sententiously, "must be a major factor in reducing efficiency."[18] A campaign conducted by the Rockefeller Institute against hookworm in Dominica had to be abandoned in the face of the apathy of the local government. The medical profession in the islands prefers to cure hookworm by injections rather than by higher wages and improved sanitation.

After hookworm, malaria. The Caribbean, from the health point of view, is a battleground of man versus mosquito. Where the Negro masses are concerned, the mosquito emerges victorious. The death rate from malaria is enormously high. In Puerto Rico an average of 30,253 cases were reported during 1932–1936.[19] Mosquito nets are a luxury, the Negro being forced to be content with the primitive method of burning green leaves in the houses; the anopheles mosquito is left to enjoy, practically undisturbed, the sanctity of his swampy breeding ground, and the Negro's house is built in unfavorable situations. "Only too frequently", says a Puerto Rican study, "houses have been built in places where the soil is very poor, or swampy, so they should not encroach on the sugar cane plantations. The information gathered indicates that more than one-fifth of the houses have swampy surroundings."[20] One of the favorite breeding areas of the mosquito is irrigated sugar lands.

Tuberculosis is another of the many plagues of the Caribbean countries, strange as it may seem in regions where winter is unknown, where the sun shines all the year round. Tuberculosis was the principal cause of death in Puerto Rico for the five-year period 1932–1936, being responsible for 15 per cent of all deaths from all causes, a rate almost unequalled in any part of the world. It affects not only urban residents, but the rural population as well, to such an extent that a comparison with the five rural states in the United States registering the highest death rates from tuberculosis gives these results: the Puerto Rican rate is more than one-half greater than that of Arizona, it is more than three times the rate of New Mexico and Tennessee, almost five times the rate of Nevada and seven times the rate of Colorado.[21]

The explanation lies in the insanitary slums which are a feature of the area. This is an English newspaper correspondent's description of the Jamaican hovel: "Strands of dried bamboo are woven round a framework of stakes and the 'room' thus formed is covered with palm thatch. There is no furniture except sacking on the earth and some sort of table to hold the oil-stove."[22] The furniture in the home of a Haitian peasant is valued at from two to fifteen dollars. Less than half of the families studied owned a bed;

37

only one-quarter owned more than a bed, chairs and a table.[23] The furniture of a Puerto Rican rural family is "scanty and of the cheapest quality, . . . a few benches, some empty boxes, a small table, one or two cots and a home-made wooden bed is about all that is seen, and in some of them, not even as much as that." Of these Puerto Rican homes, nearly nine-tenths on the sugar plantations lack bathing conveniences.[24] The lack of latrines has already been referred to. Even the names of slavery days, "barracks" and "ranges", exist to shock hypersensitive Britons who do not wish to provide grist for Hitler's mill. Commissioners from England visited such dwellings in Trinidad and found them "indescribable in their lack of elementary needs of decency." In one of these barracks three water-closets were provided to serve 48 rooms with an estimated population of 226. The closets were 150 yards from the furthest dwellings.[25] This is a description of what the Royal Commission of 1939 saw in Jamaica: "At Orange Bay the Commissioners saw people living in huts the walls of which were bamboo knitted together as closely as human hands were capable; the ceilings were made from dry crisp coconut branches which shifted their positions with every wind. The floor measured 8 feet by 6 feet. The hut was 5 feet high. Two openings served as windows, and a third, stretching from the ground to the roof, was the door. A threadbare curtain divided it into two rooms. It perched perilously on eight concrete slabs, two at each corner. In this hut lived nine people, a man, his wife and several children. They had no water and no latrine. There were two beds. The parents slept in one, and as many of the children as could hold on in the other. The rest used the floor."[26]

Many sugar plantations provided such dwellings for their workers, with or without rent. "It is hardly too

38

much to say that on some of the sugar estates the accommodation provided is in a state of extreme disrepair and thoroughly unhygienic."[27]   A well-known Englishman, C. F. Andrews, was told on a visit to British Guiana of £100,000 just voted by a British sugar company for new machinery.   When he suggested to the manager that the filthy, insanitary "ranges" should be demolished and single cottages erected in their place, he was informed that "the London directors would not give any money for such a purpose."[28]

Even Commissioners are put somewhat out of countenance by this rather too open contempt of elementary standards of decency, and have to warn short-sighted directors that "the claim of the workpeople for the common decencies of home life should be one for primary consideration, and that by maintaining the existing conditions they were providing ground for justifiable discontent."[29]   A recent official survey in Jamaica puts the size of the average room on the plantation at 640 cubic feet, with an average occupancy of two or two and one-half persons.   Light and ventilation were deficient in half, latrines were bad in nearly three-quarters, almost half needed repair; while water supply and cooking and washing facilities were conspicuously poor.[30]   Of 860 families surveyed on the Lafayette sugar plantation in Puerto Rico, there was an average of 3.5 persons per sleeping room.[31]   A similar study of families in the coffee, fruit and tobacco regions, reveals even more serious overcrowding: 5.1 occupants per sleeping room.[32]   This overcrowding is not only responsible for the high incidence of tuberculosis; it contributes to the high illegitimacy rate among Negroes characteristic of the Caribbean.

Slum clearance schemes, very admirable, exist on paper.   Let a municipality, however, attempt to translate them into action, church dignitaries and all the members of the city corporations who are owners of or have interests in slum property will veto the scheme or render it ineffective. Public health doctors, if they are good churchmen, hesitate to prosecute a church dignitary for violation of the slum ordinances, so, instead, they persecute the tenants for living in such surroundings. Not without reason did Mr. Lloyd George describe the British West Indies as "the slums of the Empire".

"A faulty diet, heavy parasitic infestation, inadequate housing, poor sanitary conditions, etc., coupled with the weariness resulting from a strenuous work, seem to reduce the rural Puerto Rican worker to a miserable physical condition which becomes more serious with age."[33] This is substantially true of the adult Negro over the area as a whole. What then of his children? Before even they are conceived, their chances are reduced, with the prospective mother half-starved and debilitated by hookworm, open to water-borne diseases. How serious the impurity of the water supply is, we can see from British Guiana. On the majority of plantations the water supplies of laborers are provided by open unprotected trenches, which are used in some cases as navigation canals for sugar punts and are thus liable to contamination by laborers and animals. To the obvious demand for artesian wells, the reply has been given that plantation laborers do not take readily to artesian well water and prefer trench water.[34].

Mention is always made of the high birth-rate in these tropical areas. Much more staggering, much more significant is the high infant mortality rate. Take the case of the British West Indies. For England and Wales the figure is 58 per 1000 live births; for Trinidad it is 120, 137 for Jamaica, 171 for Antigua, 187 for St. Kitts, 217 for Barbados. The high infant

40

mortality rate is of great value in solving to a limited extent the "surplus population" problem. In one of the municipalities covered in the sugar-cane plantation survey in Puerto Rico, the rate is 144; for Puerto Rico as a whole it is 126 per 1000 live births. For Comerio, a town in Puerto Rico, 23 per cent of all deaths in 1934 were of infants under one year of age and 43 per cent occurred prior to the fifth year, as compared with 11 and 15 per cent respectively for the same age periods in the United States. Certainly the separate figures for the Negro, the lowest paid of all laborers, are not likely to be more flattering.

The malnutrition we have already described in the case of mother and father is to be found among the children. Malnutrition is officially given as the principal cause of one-eighth of all deaths under one year for the years 1933–1936 in Dominica.[35] Diseases of the digestive system cause the deaths of three-fifths of Puerto Rican children under two years of age, clear proof of deficient nutrition.[36] Of the total deaths in Jamaica in 1935, over one-third were of infants under five years of age. One recent examination of 12,000 school children in Kingston, Jamaica, revealed that two-fifths were undernourished.[37] An examination of 1360 school children in St. Thomas in 1937–1938 disclosed that nearly one-quarter were afflicted with intestinal parasites, seven-tenths had anemia, and three-quarters suffered from malnutrition.[38] Of nearly 2800 school children examined in Dominica, about one-half were less than 10 per cent under standard weight, and one-third more than 10 per cent below standard weight for height and age.[39] A popular superstition emphasises the beautiful white teeth of the grinning Negro. Of nearly 9000 workers examined in Puerto Rico, almost half had from one to eight teeth missing, and one-seventh nine or more teeth missing. "Undoubtedly as

41

a result of the lack of economic resources, dentistry work to mend these defects was practically unknown."[40] Thirty per cent of the school children in Kingston have carious teeth.[41] Of 78,000 children examined in Haiti between 1931 and 1937, less than six per cent had all their teeth intact, slightly over 12 per cent had clean or passably clean teeth. Of another examination of more than 10,000 school children, only six per cent used toothbrushes.[42]

Government canteens for underprivileged children are today accepted in all civilized countries. A Barbados Nutrition Committee, in recommending a modest scheme for distribution by the government of some milk and "two square white biscuits" to school children, at an estimated annual gross cost of $35,000, had to admit that "the proposal is certain to be received with derision by many".[43] In the absence of any extensive scheme for the dissemination of knowledge of contraception, it is safe to assume that there are always more babies where others have come from.

The conditions described above serve to explain the large-scale exodus from the British West Indies until recent years. What opportunities were provided for Haitian and Jamaican labor by the development of sugar plantations in Cuba and the Dominican Republic, we have already seen. Barbadians and Jamaicans flocked to the banana plantations of Costa Rica. They were imported in large numbers to build the Panama Canal, seriously undercutting the white labor there, by the deliberate policy of the United States Government. They flocked to the United States, where they became doctors, lawyers, professional men, good American citizens, even though "monkey chasers" to many of their American cousins: any "Who's Who" of Harlem will indicate this. They made money and did not forget the less fortunate folk at home. "Panama money", it was called in Barbados. The average annual remittances sent to Jamaica from overseas reached $600,000.[44] In 1930 nearly one and a quarter million dollars were remitted by Barbadians abroad, a sum nearly equal to one-third of the value of Barbadian exports for that year.[45] But the collapse of sugar in Cuba, the world depression, the tightening of immigration restrictions in the American republics have closed these avenues of emigration and wealth, and have repatriated thousands of British West Indians to intensify the struggle for survival and introduce broader, more radical ideas. But emigration, at best, could be only a partial solution of the Negro problem in the Caribbean. That problem must be solved at home.

In Puerto Rico they teach families to prepare "well-balanced diets on a minimum budget". But the Negro cannot afford meat. What is the use of an anti-malaria campaign if he is forced to live in swampy surroundings? A doctor may diagnose hookworm and yet the cure can only be temporary, if the patient is too poor to buy shoes, and the government or the sugar company loath to provide adequate sanitation facilities. At the same time it must be added that plantation proprietors are at length awaking to the futility of giving a bottle of medicine to a man who needs one square meal a day. As a Nutrition Committee in British Guiana put it, thinking of the working days lost and the cost to plantations of quinine: "we are strongly of the opinion that a concerted drive against malnutrition in the East Indian and the raising of his nutritional standard of living will result in measurable benefit to the sugar industry."[46] For "East Indian" substitute Negro, and it becomes clear that what the claims of humanity have not effected, the claims of sugar may. Paris may well be worth a Mass!

43

Local hospitals are inadequate. There are insufficient beds; sleeping on the floors is not unknown; it is commonly stated that the attitude of nurses and doctors to syphilitic patients does not encourage the latter to return for treatment. Conditions are best in the urban areas, worst in the rural districts where medical facilities are most needed. A common accusation against Public Health Officers in the British colonies is that pauper patients are attended to only after those who can pay. Doctors' plates are to be seen all over the capital city of any island: the overcrowding of the medical profession in the capital means a serious dearth in the districts where doctors are most necessary. In 1934 nearly half of the doctors in Cuba were resident in Havana alone; over half of the doctors in Haiti are found in Port-au-Prince. Of the municipalities studied in the coffee, fruit and tobacco regions of Puerto Rico, it is said: "the fact that there are less professional men and, in general, fewer medical facilities in the group of 47 municipalities, is a sure indication that the economic conditions are worse in this part than in the rest of the Island."[47]

"I am emphatically of opinion", wrote the British Labor Adviser in 1938, "that one of the benefits most needed by the West Indian worker is a cheap health service."[48] The statistics given above as to the health conditions in the Caribbean make the case for island-wide medical services, free for all the indigent, overwhelming. Yet the St. Lucia branch of the British Medical Association opposed this "blanket" application of civilized ideas to backward areas as demoralizing to the Negro, who would thereby be given something for nothing.[49] No wonder that the Vice-Chairman of the British Royal Commission which visited the Caribbean in 1939 could say: "Barbados has to thank God for health, not the medical profession."[50]

44

"A land of beggars and millionaires, of flattering statistics and distressing realities . . . Uncle Sam's second largest sweat-shop."[51]   What a well-known Puerto Rican authority has said of his native home, is true of the whole Caribbean area. Uncle Sam, John Bull, Marianne; Stars and Stripes, Union Jack, Tricolour; different ways of saying the same thing, sugar. The important thing in the history of the Negro in the Caribbean is not the political flag that floats over him but the economy that strangles him. The Negro must be given a more equitable share of the wealth he produces. The sugar industry and the land that goes with it can no longer continue to be the monopoly of a few absentee companies. These, however, are political questions, and experience teaches that political questions are solved by political methods, the specific nature of which are beyond the scope of this study.

CHAPTER V

THE LAND PROBLEM AND THE NEGRO PEASANT

The unit of production in the Caribbean still betrays the main features of the slave regime. The disappearance of slavery has not meant the disappearance of the large plantation; on the contrary, the large plantation has become larger. But the emergence of a Negro peasantry in the British islands since emancipation, the tenacious struggle of the small proprietor in Martinique or the colono in Cuba to retain his land in the face of those hostile forces described in a preceding chapter, make a fascinating story in the history of the Caribbean.

We must not harbor the mistaken notion that the alternative to the plantation system with its army of landless blacks is a system of peasant proprietorship, the division of the large estate into small farms. The small-scale production of subsistence farming would be reactionary. The Haitian revolution was a mass revolt of the Negro slaves against their masters. The revolution achieved one fundamental result; it destroyed the plantation system and gave the land to the Negro masses. Today three-fifths of all Haitian peasants own their land. Land redistribution, however, is not everything. Peasant ownership, by itself, is not a solution, and by itself may even be an impediment to progress. But wisely encouraged, in conjunction with legal restrictions on the size of plantations, it forms a necessary part of any solution of the problem of the Negro in the Caribbean.

The only compensation the British abolitionists could

46

think of making to the emancipated Negro was the Bible. The planters, more wise in their generation, knew that the Negro, not solely other-worldminded, aspired to own land. All sorts of obstacles were put in the way by the local and imperial governments to prevent the purchase of land by the freed Negroes; high price of land, heavy taxes which would force the Negroes to work, and finally the importation of Indian and other contract laborers to compete with the Negroes and reduce wages. This situation did not apply to old colonies like Barbados and Antigua, where all the available land was already appropriated. Peasant proprietorship has made progress only in Trinidad, Guiana, Jamaica, and above all Grenada, which, significantly, is not a "sugar island".

In Cuba and Puerto Rico there was always the Spanish tradition of small or medium-sized farms, especially in tobacco and coffee. The "colono" or independent cultivator, mainly white, has survived American occupation, though his tenure is becoming more and more precarious every day. In the heyday of competition between the large corporations which rushed into the profitable sugar industry, small proprietors growing cane enjoyed a period of prosperity. Under the colono system the independent cultivator makes a contract with a sugar factory to deliver so much cane annually. He might own his land, or he might lease it from the sugar company. His contract would obviously be more favorable if he owned the land. The cane is ground by the company, which pays the colono a certain fixed rate. The elimination of competition which has come from the merging of companies into one industrial giant, or the disappearance, for various reasons, of rival companies, has resulted in more onerous contracts for the colono. Frequent complaints had always been made of unjust prices for the cane delivered, of unjust estimates of the saccharine content of the cane; and it is clear that in many instances the sugar company unscrupulously defrauded the colono. The growth of latifundia, above all the tremendous development of private railways owned and operated by the sugar corporations, have gradually reduced the colonos to a state of economic vassalage which becomes worse each year. The independent cultivator owning his land is forced to sell, at prices fixed by the company; he becomes a landless wage-earner, unless he prefers to lease land from the sugar company. In the present position of the Caribbean the prospects of his survival are decidedly not bright. Cuba and Puerto Rico, under American capital, are fast being reduced to the status of Barbados, one vast plantation, with the Negro's sole raison d'être to provide labor for the sugar economy.

To what extent is the system of peasant proprietorship desirable? Let us note in the first place the competence of these proprietors, the contribution they have made to Caribbean economy. The peasant soon demonstrated that the cultivation of the so-called plantation crops was not beyond him. Cocoa, for instance, is a permanent crop which requires comparatively little capital or comparatively little cultivation after it has been planted. It is therefore well suited to cultivation by peasants. The golden age of cocoa in Trinidad is the story of the rapid rise of the Negro peasantry. Of 10,000 cocoa planters in Trinidad even today, nearly 70 per cent cultivate farms of less than ten acres, and farms of less than fifty acres represent half of the land in cocoa. Coffee is another crop well suited to peasant cultivation, with the additional advantage that the peasant can grow food crops at the same time between the coffee shrubs. Coffee is the major export of Haiti; it is the chief crop cultivated by the Haitian peasant. Arrowroot in St. Vincent, nutmegs in Gre-

48

nada, limes in Dominica, have all played their part in the development of the peasantry. Long despised by white planters as a "backwoods nigger business", the success of the banana in Jamaica is to be attributed to the peasant pioneers and their successors who richly deserve the tribute paid them by Jamaica's Director of Agriculture in 1924: "It is not an industry that we owe to science or to Bureaux or to the Director of Agriculture. It had its beginning from a very modest source. It has been built up by the genius and courage and industry and capacity of the people of this colony. . . . It is the most democratic agricultural industry to be found in the West Indies. . . . It is a fact that the small man in Jamaica is the largest producer in this trade and that it is principally due to him that the banana industry has been built up to what it is today."[1] The large planters no longer despise banana cultivation, and huge corporations like the United Fruit Company and Standard Company have their tentacles stuck deep into this once lowly and despised livelihood. On an average of the years 1929–1935, these two corporations handled nearly three-quarters of the exports and together they controlled three-fifths of the acreage under bananas. But the peasants have maintained their position; holdings under five and holdings under twenty acres represent nearly one-fifth and one-half respectively of the acreage under bananas.[2]

The place of the banana in Jamaica is taken in British Guiana by rice cultivation. The vanilla of the French islands, the cotton of the Leeward Islands, both have their place in this story of the peasantry. But the peasant's greatest victory has been won with the plantation crop par excellence, sugar. It had long been assumed that sugar was beyond the scope of the backward peasant. The colono system in Cuba and Puerto Rico contradicts this assumption, while there

remains the inescapable fact that today two-fifths of
the cane in Puerto Rico, one-fourth in Martinique, and
nearly one-half in Trinidad come from small farmers.
A report to the President of the United States in 1934
disclosed that in Puerto Rico colono cane is cheaper
than cane produced on plantations; whereas company-
grown cane was produced at a cost of $5.60 per ton
in 1930–1931, colono cane cost $4.79 per ton.[3] "It is
largely as a result of the industry and hard work of
many thousands of small growers", wrote the Assistant Commissioner of Agriculture for the West Indies
in 1930, "that the cost of production of Trinidad com-
pares favourably with that in other parts of the
Empire."[4] The 125 colono farms investigated in
Puerto Rico harvested an area of 20,400 acres, thus
giving an average of only 163 acres per farm. Five-
acre farms are clearly too small to be efficient. It is
the medium-sized farm which should be encouraged.
In the words of a Puerto Rican scholar: "the need
for more than 500 acres per farm for efficiency in production has not been substantiated by facts. In view
of the unsocial distribution of income that results from
concentration of large tracts of land in the hands of
private individuals, the practice of owning more than
500 acres should be condemned."[5]

The system of peasant proprietorship is therefore
not unjustified on economic grounds. From the social
point of view, it has even stronger justification. The
plantation system lacks the ·social stability which
inevitably accompanies peasant proprietorship. The
evidence is enormous as to the relative zeal and efficiency of the Negro slave when working for himself
or for his master. Today the Negro will work his
own land, where he refuses to work for low wages.
"The small colono", writes a Puerto Rican, "is the
romantic figure of individualism in an industry con-

trolled by a handful of corporations or powerful partnerships. While farming to the sugar-cane corporation is merely a manufacturing business, it is a way of living for most colonos. The colonos constitute an element through whom a better distribution of part of the large income produced by the sugar industry is obtained."[6]

We have a sympathetic description of just how much the land means to the landless Negro in Martinique. "The acquisition of a piece of land is for the small farmer a sign of his ascent into a higher social class, the just reward of his energy and ability. Thereafter, the new landowner, known hitherto only by a country nickname, is called 'monsieur', in the first place by his wife, especially in the presence of the neighbors. On Sundays she prepares for him a white suit, suitably starched, with a starched handkerchief to adorn the top pocket. Shoes, preferably of patent leather, a Panama hat, a pair of cuffs with large cuff-links, and a watch-chain will complete the outfit. If he has a watch, the little farmer will hardly use it, accustomed as he is to telling the time by the length of the shadows. Of course his wife improves her own wardrobe, his daughters follow the European fashions and use the latest make-up. Nevertheless these people are far from being ridiculous. They are sometimes fine people, naturally distinguished, whatever their origins. And certainly the starting point of their social rise is an honorable one."[7]

Those numerous commissions, furthermore, which are a feature of British West Indian history give us a clear insight into the social merits and desirability of peasant proprietorship. As this is the burning question of the moment in the Caribbean, their opinions are worth considering in some detail. The Royal Commission of 1897 reported as follows: "The existence

51

of a class of small proprietors among the population is a source of both economic and political strength. . . . No reform affords so good a prospect for the permanent welfare in the future of the West Indies as the settlement of the labouring population on the land as small peasant proprietors." The Sugar Commission of 1929 drew a contrast between the prosperity of those colonies in which a peasantry existed and the degradation and squalor of those in which the lower classes were largely plantation laborers, and repeated: "The settlement of labourers on the land as peasant proprietors offers the best prospect of establishing a stable and prosperous economy in the West Indian colonies." Where peasant cultivation prevailed, according to a Jamaica Commission on Unemployment in 1936, conditions were comparatively favorable and there was little extreme hardship.[9] "A matter of paramount importance" is the laconic comment of the Commission sent out from England to Trinidad in 1937, recommending the extension of land settlement.[10]

The consensus of opinion (among non-owners of plantations, naturally) in favor of peasant proprietorship is overwhelming. Yet the Administrator of St. Vincent, in an address to the Legislative Council in December 1935, admitted that more than half of the privately owned land and most of the best cultivated areas were owned by some thirty plantations, while of the 2763 peasants in a population of 55,000, 95 per cent owned holdings of less than ten acres. The Government was "studying" the means of extending land settlement. Since 1899 it had been studying it and had purchased 8250 acres. Yet the Administrator "saw no easy solution of the difficulty".[11] In Barbados, three-quarters of the holdings are less than one acre. In Jamaica, more than half of the total area was comprised in 1930 in less than 1400 properties, each averaging 1000 acres.

The situation outlined above is true also of the former Spanish colonies. In 1900 a law was passed in Puerto Rico limiting farms to a maximum of 500 acres. That law has remained on the statute book, openly violated, transgressors unpunished. Only in recent months has any attempt been made to enforce it, and a commission has recently been appointed to study the question. Under Governor Tugwell, seven million dollars have been appropriated for the purchase of 200,000 acres of sugar-cane land owned by corporations, dividing them into lots of 500 acres or less, and selling them on 40-year terms. So far not a cent has been spent.[12] In 1930, sugar farms of less than twenty acres represented nearly three-quarters of the number in the island, but slightly over one-tenth of the acreage in farms. Farms of 500 acres or more, less than one per cent of the total farms, occupied nearly one-third of all the area of Puerto Rico included in farms.[13] Of 247,000 workers engaged in Puerto Rican agriculture, less than one-fifth own the land they till. The number of farms in Cuba declined more than one-third between 1899 and 1935; the percentage of cane produced by free colonos declined from 27 in 1929 to 10 in 1933.[14]

Why the recommendations of the past have been ignored is simple in the extreme: land settlement is contrary to the interest of the planter. Three centuries ago he destroyed the small white farmer; today he is determined to destroy the small farmer, black, white, or brown. As the Sugar Commission to the British islands in 1929 recognized: "if they (the planters) encouraged action which, in their belief, must tend to diminish their labour supply, they would be cutting away the branch upon which they sit."[15] Only an explosion makes the planters realize that these repeated recommendations in the past are not platonic. While the Secretary of State for the Colonies in

England was telling Parliament in 1938 of $110,000 spent on land settlement in Jamaica in the past year, the unemployed and underpaid Negroes of the island went on strike and began rioting. Immediately the governor of the colony allotted $2,500,000, later increased to $3,250,000, to land settlement schemes.

The case for peasant proprietorship is clear. The Pan-American Labor Conference which met at Havana in 1939 called for the destruction of the large estates. They included in this Cuba but not Puerto Rico, Haiti but not Jamaica, the "independent" republics but not the dependent colonies. The destruction of the large estates is not a Cuban or Dominican problem but a Caribbean one.

We must not, however, be romantic about this question of peasant proprietorship. Peasant ownership, by itself, is no solution of the agricultural problem of the Caribbean. Haiti is the glaring example. The average holding is small, from three to six acres, and lots of one-fifth of an acre are not uncommon. The method of cultivation is primitive in the extreme. The plough is unknown. A hoe and cutlass, valued at $1.20, represent the sum total of the peasant's instruments of production.[16] He is ignorant of questions of fertility, selection of seeds and plants, protection against insects and disease. His is essentially a subsistence agriculture, a pre-capitalist economy in which wages are unknown. To the primitive methods of coffee cultivation and preparation is to be ascribed the earthy flavor of Haitian coffee which makes it unpopular in the world market. The preparation of the soil is the task of the family or an organization known as the "coumbite", a primitive method of co-operation which has been described by Dr. Simpson as "one of the most popular, most beneficial, and most durable of Haitian institutions."[17] The Haitian peasant is poor,

54

miserably poor. In the expressive creole dialect of the country, he is a "toutiste": he does everything for himself. The annual incomes of peasants in the district of Plaisance have been estimated at from 40 to 300 dollars, with the maximum figure rare. It is this poverty which has encouraged the Haitian to emigrate to the "superior" opportunities of field work in the sugar industry in Cuba and the Dominican Republic. The Haitian peasant owns his land. But that is only half the battle. For peasant ownership to succeed, the peasant must be taught and educated, and his primitive instincts corrected. For failure to do this the mulatto overlords of Haiti bear as great a responsibility as the white foreign overlords elsewhere in the Caribbean who have consistently opposed peasant ownership.

"The experience of a large number of countries", says a West Indian student, "entitles us to say that, given adequate facilities, a system of advice and instruction, and centralised processing and marketing, peasants can compete effectively with any plantation system."[18] In the extension of co-operative methods lies the best hope for improvement of peasant cultivation. The establishment of co-operatives has made some headway in the Caribbean. Co-operatives mean improved methods of production, improved methods of marketing, above all organization for the obtaining of credit—to reduce the stranglehold in which colonos find themselves, from the necessity of taking advances at such usurious rates as banks and sugar companies care to charge. There is a co-operative of vegetable growers, another for the disposal of cotton, still another of colonos in Puerto Rico. The outstanding example of co-operativism in the Caribbean— admittedly in a peculiar form—is the Jamaica Banana Producers' Association, the overwhelming number of whose members are small farmers. Co-operation is making progress in British Guiana, where a Small Farmers Committee has published an invaluable report emphasizing not only the need of redistributing idle private land among peasants in five- or seven-acre plots, on easy credit terms, but of improving peasant cultivation by means of district agricultural co-operative societies.[19]

This is not to say that there are no organizations in the Caribbean devoted to the study of improved methods. Large sums of money are devoted annually to research for improving production, increasing efficiency, controlling plant diseases. Every island has its Agricultural Department, its experimental stations. The peasant benefits little from this research. Trinidad has a magnificent College of Tropical Agriculture where colored students are, to put it mildly, unwelcome, though they cannot be completely discouraged. This college is of as little benefit to the Trinidad peasant farmer as Oxford University. Much work remains to be done in the future in this question of expert advice to the peasants. The institute run by the Haitian Government at Damien is at present trying to correct the evils of the past, but its importance is clearly still to be realized. The fiscal year 1939–1940 saw a decline in the expenditures of the Haitian Government of less than four per cent. Yet the budget of the all-important Department of Agriculture and Labor was cut 36 per cent. Advice to peasant farmers, improvement of their methods and organization, depend upon a definite settled policy with reference to peasant proprietorship. This ultimately is a political question; the future course of the struggle between planter and peasant depends on changes in the political structure of the islands.

CHAPTER VI

THE MIDDLE CLASS AND THE RACIAL PROBLEM

In the early years of slavery the social divisions were extremely simple: at the top of the pyramid was the small handful of whites—owners and overseers; the base was the Negro slaves. Juxtaposition of the two races soon produced a third class. The slave had no legal rights; if the male slave was in most instances denied the privilege of marrying, the female slave was denied the right of refusing access to her bed on the part of her owner or his overseer. The refusal of sexual intercourse with a white overseer was equivalent to mutiny. It was no uncommon thing for a planter to line up his slave girls before his guest who was invited to take his choice for the night. The slave women were defenceless under the regime of slavery, and the white man's preoccupation with his slave women, his neglect of his white wife, and the tolerant attitude to concubinage were responsible for no small part of the disgraceful cruelty of white women to slave girls.

This picture, true as it is of the Caribbean as a whole, varied in different islands. The Frenchman and Spaniard, lacking, then as now, the cruder aspect of racial prejudice which, then as now, distinguishes the Anglo-Saxon, in many instances married his concubine. But concubine or wife, intercourse with slave women produced an increasingly large colored or mulatto element in all the islands. In the eighteenth century the British Leeward Islands made a profitable business out of rearing quadroon and octoroon girls and

57

sending them to Dutch Guiana to be sold for the Caribbean harem.

It was customary for white planters to free their mulatto offspring, though the tendency was stronger among the Latin races than among the English. During the slavery regime this mulatto class, with a few free blacks, came to occupy a more and more important position. It was the mulattoes of French Saint Domingue who began the revolution in that colony demanding the political equality with whites to which their wealth and education entitled them. It was said of this class of people in Jamaica in 1827 that they were men of property, who compared favorably with the impecunious whites. In Barbados they were superior to many of the whites in refinement, morals, education and energy, and, significantly for the future, the governor wrote to the home government in 1833, on the eve of emancipation: "you will see a large policy in present circumstances in bringing these castes forward. They are a sober, energetic and loyal race; and I could equally depend on them if need came, against either slaves or white militia."

This intermediate caste in slave society despised the black side of its ancestry. The mulatto woman preferred to be the mistress of a white man than to marry a black. Like the similar group in New Orleans and Charleston, they occupied a privileged position before emancipation. With the prestige of white blood in their veins, they refused to do laboring work. They despised the "no-good niggers", and where, as in some cases, they themselves owned slaves, they were as vicious and tyrannical as the poor whites. Some few, educated by an indulgent white father, eventually became owners of land; others, more numerous, settled in the urban areas and became artisans, small clerks, etc. They formed the humble beginnings of the colored and black middle class in the Caribbean.

Emancipation gave a decided stimulus to this class. Making rapid progress, they learned to read and write; they resorted to retail trade and commerce; tilling their small plots judiciously, they increased their ownership of land and made money in cocoa or bananas. Desiring above all things "independence" for their children, they sent the latter to European Universities where they became doctors and lawyers and returned to their native land to monopolize the professions. The colored middle class had arrived.

Today they occupy an important position in the Caribbean structure. They are concentrated in the towns, where they are easily distinguished by their lighter skin. Even in Haiti, according to Dr. Price Mars, while 80 per cent of the country people are black, from 40 to 50 per cent of the city folk are light in colo:.[1] Where the colored middle classes are to be seen on the countryside, they figure as landed gentry.

They are, too, essentially professional people. Squeezed out of retail trade by the waves of Chinese, Portuguese, Syrians and Jews who have in that order invaded the Caribbean, and who today control the rum shops, dry goods stores, groceries and laundries, the colored middle class virtually monopolize the professions of medicine and law in the British and French islands. Even in Cuba and Puerto Rico their importance in these professions is great. They dominate the lower ranks of the civil service bureaucracy; they are to be found in the legislative councils; they are gradually pushing their way into the higher ranks of the government. One of the most famous Chief Justices in Barbados was a poor mulatto boy who rose to be Sir Conrad Reeves. A Negro of Dominica was Chief Justice of the island in 1873, Solicitor General and Attorney General of the Leeward Islands between 1881 and 1886, Registrar and Provost Marshal of Dominica from 1886 to 1891. Today by far the

59

dominant figure on the Trinidad scene, a prominent lawyer, King's Counsel, Knight of the British Empire, is a colored man, the legal representative of the oil companies. A Barbadian Negro, Arthur Barclay, became President of Liberia in 1904.

In training and in outlook these middle classes are European. They retain little or no trace of their African origin except the color of their skin. Some have been educated at Oxford, the Sorbonne, Madrid. They are colored Europeans, in dress (carried to such absurd lengths as wearing the dark colors and heavy-weight suits of the colder mother countries), in tastes, in opinions and in aspirations. They often marry white women, English, French, Spanish, Canadian and American. When they go "home" every four years to enjoy a well-earned holiday they imply by "home" not Africa, but England, France, even Spain. In the British islands they save or borrow to see the pageantry of England at the time of a coronation or jubilee. The visit of a Prince of Wales, the honeymoon of a royal couple find them ready to display their loyalty to the throne, their affection for the mother country. They remain profoundly ignorant of the neighboring islands, each group basking in its splendid isolation. They would as soon think of going to Timbuctoo as of spending a holiday in Haiti.

Thirty years ago Sir Harry Johnston launched a bitter attack on the Haitian middle class which is typical of the Western attitude to that country. What he condemned in Haiti is equally true today of the Negro middle class all over the Caribbean. "Haiti possesses one of the most magnificent floras in the world and a wonderful display of bird-life. Do you suppose any Haitian knows or cares anything about the trees, flowers, or fruit, beautiful or useful, of his own country; the birds, the fish, the butterflies, the rocks, minerals, rainfall, or wind force? Not one. And yet these same men amongst the two hundred thousand educated people know a good deal about the landscapes of France, England, Germany and Italy; can quote with appreciative delight the nature studies of Tennyson; admire the art of Corot and Daubigny; and have even heard of Turner. The amazing beauty of their own country is only apparent to them when their attention is called to it by utter strangers; and then they put forward quotations from foreign writers on Haitian scenery as an excuse for their political shortcomings or financial defalcations. They know all about the nightingale and nothing of the Haitian warblers. In their poetry they refer to the eagle and swan (completely absent from their sphere), but never to the frigate-bird or flamingo."[2]

In the days of slavery the role of the mulatto concubine was to inform against conspiracies of the field slaves, in the Caribbean as in the United States, while the free people of color, as a class, served as a social barrier between the slaves on the one hand and the slaveowners on the other. In the present society of the Caribbean the role of the people of color is by and large to collaborate, wittingly or no, with the dominant whites. The attitude of the majority of the colored middle class to the black workers is one of open contempt. What an English observer has written of Jamaica is true of all the islands: "the Jamaican bourgeoisie knows even less about the people than the English bourgeoisie about its proletariat."[3] They are adamant in their refusal to countenance any extension of the franchise to "the barefooted man" who, they say sagely, is not yet ready for such a boon. No one in the British West Indies talks so glibly of the "lazy" black as his colored brother.

The colored middle class, in fact, except in the areas

61

where whites predominate, are in a privileged political position. In Haiti, the ruling mulatto elite dominates the country economically, politically and socially. In the British West Indies high property qualifications disfranchise all but a handful of colored and white voters. In Trinidad one must earn over $300 a year before he can be registered as a voter; the agricultural laborer gets 25 cents a day. Prospective members of the Legislative Council must own real estate to the value of $10,000 or derive an annual income of $1000 therefrom. This is true, with variations, for all the British islands, with the exception of Jamaica, which has the 10-shilling vote (all chauffeurs paying a tax of two and a half dollars). Consider the results. The percentage of voters in Trinidad is 6.6 of the total population; in Jamaica 5.5; in Barbados 3.4; in Antigua 3; in British Guiana 2.9; in St. Lucia 2.2.[4] The privilege of voting, of membership in the Legislative Councils is restricted to the handful of whites and a fraction of the colored middle class. In the recent uprisings in the British West Indies the colored middle class, some of them working as clerks and salesmen for $20 a month, rushed to volunteer for service against the black strikers, or, as an English writer, referring to Trinidad, put it, "to learn how to defend the interests of the class they enter against the class they hope they have left."[5]

The racial situation in the Caribbean is radically different from the racial situation in the United States and is thus rather incomprehensible to the native of the United States, black or white. It should first be clearly understood that there is no overt legal discrimination. The islands know neither Jim Crow nor lynching; there are neither separate schools, separate theaters, separate restaurants or special seats in public conveyances. Cases of rape of white women are unknown, and we have the testimony of an ex-governor of Jamaica as to the safety of white women, anywhere at any time. White, brown and black meet in the same churches in which pews, at a price, can be obtained by one and all. Graves of whites, browns and blacks are seen side by side in the cemeteries. The declaration of fundamental rights proclaimed by the Constituent Assembly of Cuba in 1940 may be taken as indicative of the legal situation in the Caribbean: "All Cubans are equal before the law. The Republic recognises no privileges. All discrimination because of sex, race, color, or class, or other affront to human dignity is declared illegal and punishable."

The racial consciousness which permeates the American Negro is also not found in the islands. This is a constant source of surprise and even exasperation to the American Negro visitor or student, who goes to the islands with his clichés and his prejudices, seeking for any violations of his own code of racial solidarity. It is annoying, for instance, to find the term "Negro" little used and almost an epithet of abuse or contempt, at least among intimate friends. The Haitians consider themselves "blacks", not Negroes. It is difficult, too, for the American Negro to realize that the term "colored" signifies a distinct group in the Caribbean. It is an old definition, dating back to the days of slavery. The English islands spoke of the "people of color"; in the French they were "gens de couleur"; in the Spanish "gente de color". One is not a mulatto in Cuba or Puerto Rico—one might be "pardo", or "moreno", or "trigueño", indicating different shades of brown.

If in the United States one drop of Negro blood makes a man a Negro, in the islands one is white or not according to the color of one's skin. If in the United States one is classified as a Negro if his Negro ancestry

63

goes back to the fourth generation, then in the Caribbean one is considered white in the second generation. A common remark in the British West Indies of colored schoolboys to a companion of lighter skin whom they consider uppish is: "go home and look at your grandmother". There is a similar saying in Puerto Rico, in a popular song which says: "and your grandmother, where is she?"

Of overt legal discrimination, therefore, there is none in the Caribbean. Economic differences prevent the color question of the United States from arising. Only on the social level does racial prejudice present itself, but there in a radical form. A white skin, in a society still obsessed economically and therefore culturally by the slave tradition, is an indication of social status and the best passport to political influence. The nearer one is to the coveted white skin, the more likely is one to be accepted in society. If one is not fortunate enough to have a white skin, the next best thing is a partner with a white skin. Married to a white woman, a young Negro rapidly ascends the ladder of success. How could it be otherwise? If the white skin means superiority, then the white woman, in the interest of white prestige, must be given an opportunity to live in a way and on a standard compatible with white dignity.

It is this high market value of a white skin, in addition to the stigma of past slavery and its consequences, which is responsible for those color distinctions for which the islands are notorious. These distinctions have the greatest effect in the lack of cohesion which exists among the middle classes. We have a picture of these color distinctions of middle class society in the British West Indies, drawn by a native Trinidadian. It may be taken as indicative of the colored middle class over the whole area. "Between the brown-skinned middle class and the black there is a continual

64

rivalry, distrust and ill-feeling, which, skilfully played upon by the European people, poisons the life of the community. Where so many crosses and colors meet and mingle, the shades are naturally difficult to determine and the resulting confusion is immense. There are the nearly-white hanging on tooth and nail to the fringes of white society, and these, as is easy to understand, hate contact with the darker skin far more than some of the broader-minded whites. Then there are the browns, intermediates, who cannot by any stretch of imagination pass as white, but who will not go one inch toward mixing with people darker than themselves. And so on, and on, and on. Associations are formed of brown people who will not admit into their number those too much darker than themselves, and there have been heated arguments in committee as to whether such and such a person's skin was fair enough to allow him or her to be admitted, without lowering the tone of the institution. Clubs have been known to accept the daughter and mother, who were fair, but to refuse the father, who was black. A dark-skinned brother in a fair-skinned family is sometimes the subject of jeers and insults and open intimations that his presence is not required at the family social functions. Fair-skinned girls who marry dark men are often ostracised by their families and given up as lost. There have been cases of fair women who have been content to live with black men but would not marry them. Should the darker man, however, have money or position of some kind, he may aspire, and it is not too much to say that in a West Indian colony the surest sign of a man's having arrived is the fact that he keeps company with people lighter in complexion than himself. Remember, finally, that the people most affected by this are people of the middle class who, lacking the hard contact with realities of the masses and unable

65

to attain to the freedoms of a leisured class, are more than all types of people given to trivial divisions and subdivisions of social rank and precedence."[6]   Prospective brides look for light-skinned men.   They pray for "light" children, who might marry white.   Expectant mothers abstain from coffee or chocolate.   As the saying goes in Martinique, one who has reached the dining-room should not go back to the kitchen.

For Haiti, Dr. Price Mars, himself a Negro, writes on this subject: "an enormous difference exists between the peasant majority, whose life is essentially bound up with the cultivation of the land according to methods that are ancient and obsolete, and the small minority engaged in business, industry and public office in the cities.   Their economic interests are apparently divergent.   One produces, the other buys either to consume or to resell.   They dress differently—one is rigged out in cotton and goes barefooted while the other is attired in the latest European style.   Finally their mentalities are distinct; whereas one group is hardly emerging from a primitive condition, the other is prey to all the troubled heritage of the western civilizations. Such an immense difference exists between these two categories of Haitian society that they seem to belong to two different worlds."[7]

The middle class elite in the Caribbean is Christian or free-thinking, while the masses still cling to ancient beliefs and rites, as the "voodoo" of Haiti, the "shango" of Trinidad, the "pocomania" of Jamaica. The Haitian masses speak a debased patois, the colored middle class perfect French; the two classes would not understand each other but for the fact that the use of "creole" in ordinary everyday speech is universal. The main aim of the Caribbean colored middle class is to forget their African origin.   The solitary exception is Cuba, where there exists the Society for Afro-Cuban

66

Studies, whose founder and inspirer was a white lawyer and author, Dr. Fernando Ortíz, the leading scholar of the Caribbean. Many colored Cubans are associated in this Society which has been doing excellent work, of both scholarly and practical value, in showing the contributions, material and cultural, of the Negro element to Cuban society.

The question on everyone's lips in the Caribbean today is what effect will the closer military ties with the United States have on the racial situation in the islands. Latin America, with its large mulatto or mestizo population, will watch closely the effects of this intrusion on the morale of a people already sensitive on questions of race. White American tourists in Havana show consternation on seeing the "racial democracy" of Cuba. Racial prejudice was always infinitesimal in the Spanish colonies, especially in Puerto Rico, which was more a military outpost than a plantation colony. But changes have occurred under American rule and influence, and American racial attitudes have begun to exercise their usual disruptive influence.

The British Royal Commission of 1939 has called for an organized effort to prevent the extension of race prejudice. Exactly what that means is not clear. The employment of Southerners and South Africans in the Trinidad oilfields has resulted in a noticeable increase in racial tension. Excessive emphasis on the racial issue is as dangerous in the black man as it is in the white. The Communist Party in Cuba have been clamoring for a black belt and self-determination of the Negro in the areas where he dominates. Those areas, however, are essentially the areas of sugar and of alien laborers. The Negro in Cuba, the mulatto in the Dominican Republic, are being undercut by cheap black labor from Haiti and Jamaica. Obviously, therefore, one must be wary of too sweeping a racial

67

interpretation of Caribbean history. But there is dynamite in the racial situation. Essentially the difference between capital and labor in the Caribbean is a difference between black and white, and the significant increase of racial consciousness which followed on the Italo-Ethiopian war is a portent which will bear watching. It is a healthy sign, however, that attempts to play off Indians against Negroes in the British colonies have so far not succeeded.

There is great uneasiness among British and French West Indians that closer ties with the United States will involve the introduction of American racial attitudes. God save the "local white" from a "grandmother clause"! But racial discrimination will fall heaviest on the black masses. "Incidents" are increasing and even the English press is getting restless. The American authorities in the new bases have protested against the system by which a white offender might be arrested by a black policeman and fined by a black magistrate. Hotels frequented by American tourists have generally in the past refused to serve people of color, and the American soldiers are today insisting that Negroes should be excluded from public bars where Americans are being served. It is reported that the British Government has asked the United States Government not to send Negroes to the new bases. Recalling the Virgin Islands and Puerto Rico, the explanation could hardly be, as the N.A.A.C.P. suggests, that the example of qualified American Negroes filling high positions will arouse too great ambitions on the part of the underprivileged British Negro. There are such qualified Negroes all over the British West Indies. The Negro masses of the Caribbean know nothing of the economics of Hitlerism. To their simple minds Hitlerism means two things: brutal tyranny and racial prejudice. If the American view

68

of race is to become part of the lease-lend program, then for them it will be keeping out Beelzebub by Beelzebub, or the alternatives of Tweedledum and Tweedledee. As Shakespeare remarked, "there is small choice 'twixt rotten apples", and the intrusion of new brands of race prejudice into the Caribbean will provoke serious social and political repercussions.

CHAPTER VII

NATIVE EDUCATION

The author of a history of Jamaica in 1740 wrote as follows: "Learning is here at the lowest ebb: there is no public school in the whole island, neither do they seem fond of the thing: several large donations have been made for such uses, but have never taken effect. The office of a teacher is looked upon as contemptible and no gentleman keeps company with one of that character; to read, write, and cast accounts is all the education they desire, and even these are but scurvily taught. A man of any parts or learning that would employ himself in that business, would be despised and starve. The gentlemen whose fortunes can allow it, send their children to Great Britain, where they have the advantage of a polite and generous education."

If this was the situation as far as whites were concerned, the situation of the black slaves was worse. Based on slavery like the ancient states of Greece, Caribbean society did not reproduce the gifts of Greece to the world. As Sir James Stephen, the abolitionist, wrote of the British slave colonies in 1831: "there is no civilized society on earth so entirely destitute of learned leisure, of literary and scientific intercourse and even of liberal recreations." There was one exception in the Caribbean. The history of Cuba in the nineteenth century is full of the names of famous scholars and writers, who in some cases enjoyed a European reputation: Varela, Saco, Martí, to mention only a few. One of them, Menéndez, one of the outstanding educators of his time, was a Negro. During the colonial regime Antonio Medina was to the Negro in Cuba what José de la Luz y Caballero was to the white. But the education of the blacks was not viewed with favor. Strangely enough, the majority of schoolmasters in the thirty-nine schools which existed in La Habana in 1793 were Negroes. But when a free Negro woman asked permission in 1827 to open a school for colored girls, she was refused; and to the request of a Negro in 1865 for authorization to open a night school for adult Negroes, who would be taught grammar, geography, drawing and history, the Governor of the island asked him "whether he did not know that such knowledge was prohibited to Negroes." At the time of the abolition of slavery in Cuba in 1886, not only were Negro children debarred from schools in the interior, but in the capital, Havana, with a population of 400,000 Negroes, there were only four schools maintained by the municipality for the education of Negro children.[1] In Haiti, to the credit of King Christophe, it must be said that he realized the value and necessity of education, and with the aid of British abolitionists some few schools were opened, but the vicissitudes of revolution and the poverty of the country prevented any real attempt to grapple with the education problem. As early as 1770 equality of education was decreed in Puerto Rico for whites and mulattoes, while one of the most distinguished educators in the history of the island, Rafael Cordero, was a Negro, after whom a street in San Juan is named.

The development of education for the Negro in the Caribbean was, and is, of slow growth. As in the United States, missionaries were the pioneers. The Mico Charity continued the good work in Jamaica, and the Canadian Mission to the Indians, together with the prominence of denominational education, still emphasize today the part played by religious orders in the educational system and secular lack of interest in education. The percentage of illiteracy in the area is still enormously high. The progress made in Cuba is striking, and is due largely to the strong desire of the Negroes themselves, in spite of discrimination and opposition. In 1865 the percentage of illiteracy among Negroes was 95; it was reduced to 72 in 1889, 54 in 1907, and 46 in 1917. The percentage of illiteracy in Haiti is still over 80, in Trinidad 43, and in British Guiana as high as 60. The excuse offered is the large East Indian population in these two colonies, and the objection of these Indians to education of their women. The excuse is quite inadequate for the area as a whole, where there are no Indian women. Another excuse is offered in Puerto Rico, where illiteracy, 80 per cent in 1899, was still 35 per cent in 1935. Quite gratuitously, the Commissioner of Education, in reply to a letter merely asking for reports of the Department of Education, wrote blaming the density of population in Puerto Rico: "In my opinion the density of our population is the cause of many of our evils. There are over 500 people to the square mile, and the means to support them are very slender. With such a density, the United States would have, to be exact, 1,513,-394,500 inhabitants, without including Alaska and the insular possessions. The above will explain why the schools of the Island have not been able to enroll more than 45 per cent of the children of school age. Education is but a reflection of the pitiful conditions in which our people must struggle and live. Efforts to educate our adults must also suffer from lack of proper means."

The basic reason for this illiteracy is the poverty, the excessive inequality of incomes, the political weakness of the masses. But this is not the whole explanation. It is the deliberate policy of planters and governments to keep the people ignorant and unlettered. In the words of one planter: "give them some education in the way of reading and writing, but no more. Even then I would say educate only the bright ones; not the whole mass. If you do educate the whole mass of the agricultural population, you will be deliberately ruining the country. . . . Give the bright ones a chance to win as many scholarships as they can; give the others three hours' education a day . . . but if you keep them longer you will never get them to work in the fields. If you want agricultural labourers and not dissatisfaction, you must not keep them longer."[2] Another planter was asked whether he did not think it would be more satisfactory that children under twelve should be sent to school rather than begin work as soon as they were able, to which he replied that education "would be of no use to them". Were they then to be without education at all? "As long as this is an agricultural country", was his reply, "of what use will education be to them if they had it?"[3]

In these candid words we have planter mentality over the area. Education means discontent, and planters must have their labor supply. Much of the lighter work on plantations is done by children under twelve, and planters want to make sure of their child labor. In British Guiana an Education Ordinance exists requiring children to attend school up to the age of fourteen. The same ordinance prohibits children from being employed during school hours if below the age of twelve. Thus, while the Education Department can prosecute the parent for the non-attendance of a child between the ages of twelve and fourteen, it cannot prosecute the employer for the employment, although the employment might be the cause of absence from school.[4] A special Education Commission, sent out to the colonies in 1931 from England, has even justified child labor: "we appreciate the argument of those who see in compulsion an instrument for abolish-

73

ing child labour on the estates. But while accepting the desirability of such abolition we think it is possible to overestimate its extent and its evils. It is for the most part confined to the sugar and, at certain seasons, cotton estates. The conditions are not comparable to those of factory labour under European urban industrial conditions, and we are not convinced that children 12 years old are necessarily worse off under these conditions than they would be in the overcrowded badly staffed schools which the introduction of compulsion without heavy additional expenditures would perpetuate and extend."[5]

Against this background consider the inadequacy of education in the Caribbean. In 1933 half a million children in Cuba, or well over half of the population of school age, were not enrolled in schools. Nearly two-thirds of the enrolment in the elementary schools were in the first two grades. Enrolment is highest in the provinces of Havana and Matanzas, lowest in the areas of highest population, Camaguey and Oriente, the sugar areas of the island, where the Negroes predominate. In 1935 the province of Oriente could boast of only one-sixth of the libraries in the island and less than two per cent of the volumes. The expenditure on education was $1.49 per capita in 1935, or $13.90 per child enrolled in the elementary schools—less than one-third the sum spent in the poorest state in the United States. Only five per cent of the adolescent population in Cuba have an opportunity to continue their education in a public school for more than six years.[6]

In Puerto Rico only 44 per cent of the school population is enrolled, and of this number half are enrolled on half time only. Of the rural schools four-fifths have facilities for grades one to three only. Slightly more than one-quarter of the enrolments in 1937–1938 were

74

in grades four through eight. In 1919–1920 only two per cent of the school children were enrolled in regular high schools, in 1937–1938 less than five per cent. The per capita expenditure per child in Puerto Rico based on current expense and average daily attendance, is $24.21, less than in the poorest states of the United States; two-fifths of the island's budget is assigned to education. Superficially this proportion is high; the explanation is clearly that total revenues must be increased. How? Tax the sugar corporations adequately, to provide education for the children of sugar laborers. Occupying the lowest rung of the economic ladder, the Negro gets inevitably less education than his white compatriot. The Negro enrolment for all schools in Puerto Rico is nearly 17 per cent; for high schools less than 20 per cent; for elementary rural schools (the Negro is essentially an agricultural laborer) 14 per cent; for what are called second unit rural schools 16 per cent.[7] Remember that the Negroes represent between one-third and one-half of the total population.

In the British islands not more than three-fifths of the population of school-going age is enrolled. Compulsory education exists—on paper. The expenditure per child is one-sixth of the sum spent in England. In Trinidad, perhaps the most advanced colony educationally, less than one-tenth of the revenue is allotted to education, and the average salary of elementary school teachers is a paltry fifteen to twenty dollars a month, about the wage of an unskilled worker on the oil-fields if he is employed every day.

The education provided is furthermore woefully unsuited to local conditions. Along liberal lines, little attention is paid to vocational education, and the Caribbean has produced no Booker T. Washington. It is really education for the sons of the middle classes, not for the sons of agricultural laborers. One Haitian naively justified the imitation of the French educational system on the ground that it had produced such excellent results in France. The education of Barbados is severely classical at the secondary level, and Barbadian classical scholars, white and colored, have attained well-deserved fame in England.

Consider the subjects on which the Trinidad open scholarship to England is awarded: English Political History, a special period of English Political History, European History, Greek History, English Colonial History, English Economic History; Latin text-books, translation, composition and Roman History; French text-books, translation and composition; Spanish text-books, translation and composition; two plays of Shakespeare, a play of Chaucer, two papers on a special period of English literature, one on specially assigned books, the other general. English examinations, set by English examiners in England, are the rule. In one notorious instance an essay was assigned on "a day in winter", to students to whom winter was only "hiemps" or "hiver" or "invierno". In broad outline the picture is true for all the British colonies, and their secondary education is not free. Even on the elementary level the education is inclined to be academic and literary. Local history is ignored, the history of Europe takes first place. As Cuba's great scholar, José Martí, wrote in 1887: "The head of a giant is being placed on the body of an ant. And every day . . . the head is being increased and the body decreased."

The majority of schools in the islands are located in the urban centers, few in the rural areas where they are most needed. Take the case of Haiti. Maurice Dartigue, then Director of Rural Education, now Minister of Public Instruction, writes: "In addition to the fact that 85 to 90 per cent of the population of school age lives in rural communities, primary education in the towns receives more money from the budget of the Republic than rural education, though the former embraces fewer pupils and far fewer schools, while giving an education far less rich and varied." Only 10 per cent of the school-going population in the rural areas is enrolled. Little attention is paid to girls. One-third of the rural schools are for girls, and enrolment of girls represents only one-quarter of the total.[8] Rural education is as yet in its infancy in the British islands, and the Puerto Rico Reconstruction Administration is trying to supplement the deficiency by training specially selected laborers. But there is no point to rural education, however, if under the present economic system the Negro is doomed to remain a landless wage-earner.

In one respect the former Spanish colonies are, in the field of education, superior to the British and French islands. Cuba has a University dating back to the early eighteenth century, and its importance in the life of Cuba today is well attested by the high reputation of its Schools of Medicine and Dentistry, whilst some of the greatest names in tropical medicine are Cuban. The Dominican Republic too boasts of a University; so does Puerto Rico, a credit to American control. The University of Puerto Rico, with its agricultural experiment station, is doing excellent research on sociological and economic problems, while the School of Tropical Medicine, under the supervision of Columbia University, has been producing some of the most valuable studies on agricultural regions and workers in the Caribbean. Haiti possesses a School of Medicine and a School of Law dating back to the second half of the nineteenth century, and since 1920 a University. But consider closely the situation in Cuba. The emphasis is essentially on law, medicine

77

and pedagogy. Of the total enrolment of nearly 7000, Negroes represent a little over 8 per cent, Negro women one-ninth of all women enrolled. In the school of medicine, about 10 per cent are Negroes; in dental surgery 15 per cent; pedagogy, 10 per cent; civil law, 6 per cent. On the other hand only 3 per cent of the enrolment in political, social and economic sciences are Negroes; of the sciences, chemical and natural, electrical and agricultural engineers, chemical and agricultural experts, only 3 per cent are Negroes.[9] Still the same slave mentality, the same concern with an independent "profession". In fairness to them we must ask, however, what good it would do a Negro in the Caribbean to become an agricultural sugar engineer? Imagine an American sugar corporation in Cuba or Puerto Rico employing Negroes in such a capacity!

It should be stated here that racial segregation in the educational system in the Caribbean does not exist. In the elementary schools in the British colonies, the children are all Negro or colored; white children go to private schools. On the secondary level all over the area, whites, Negroes, mulattoes, Indians, Chinese sit side by side, competing equally in the classroom and on the playing fields. A pernicious innovation in recent years in Trinidad is the offer of a scholarship, at the instigation of a high educational administrator (white) in Trinidad, by an English "public" school to boys of pure European descent only. If three hundred Americans find jobs as teachers of English in Puerto Rico, and Manchester has been better able to hold its own in British West Indian markets with its exports of Bachelors of Arts than with its textiles, Negroes and mulattoes are not excluded and draw the same pay as whites. The present faculty of Queen's Royal College, the government secondary school in Trinidad, is about one-third colored, an indication of the role of

the native people in education. One of the professors
of pedagogy in the University of Havana is a woman
of color; the head of the Social Science Department in
the University of Puerto Rico is the daughter of Puerto
Rico's grand old man of color, and her husband is also
a member of the faculty.

What, in contrast, can the British and French islands
show in the field of higher education? Nothing but
island scholarships to England, Rhodes scholarships
for Jamaica, and Codrington College in Barbados,
affiliated to Durham University in England, where one
can study classics and theology. The Rhodes scholarships emphasize social status. The Negro is thereby
automatically excluded, but the larger percentage of
winners of the island scholarships are Negro and
colored boys. As in Cuba, the majority of these
scholars study law and medicine in England, while
British West Indian students in the United States take
to medicine and dentistry. After a rule of, in some
cases, three centuries, there is no University in the
French or British West Indies. Future doctors go to
the School of Tropical Medicine and Hygiene in London, there to be taught the control of malaria and
typhoid by men who may never have seen a case of
either, while the School of Tropical Medicine in Puerto
Rico lies next door, without any language difficulties
to overcome. What a field there is for a University
in the British West Indies, with a School of Tropical
Medicine, drawing sustenance from the very soil,
ministering directly to the needs of the people!
Demands are being voiced today for such a University. Those demands are meeting with opposition
from individual islands, each one jealous of the other,
and the Royal Commission of 1939 never bothered
even to mention the subject. A University however
will be of no use if it attempts merely to reproduce the

79

curriculum of Oxford or London, and fails to take account of the particular needs to be filled in the islands.

So much for education. What then of the arts? French Martinique can boast only of being the birth place of Napoleon's consort, Josephine, and the eldest Dumas, and so take some pride in the literary achievements of the great novelist. In the British West Indies there is little imaginative literature published and writers and artists of any talent generally go abroad. Claude McKay, of American fame, is a Jamaican by birth. The only major accomplishment in the field of native culture in the British islands is the "calypso" of Trinidad. The calypso is a popular song, spontaneously composed, with a refrain, sung at the annual carnivals. These songs, some vulgar and banal in the extreme, have become a vehicle for social philosophies, for satirical quips on men and matters of local and world importance. Advice to young women that it is better to be a young man's slave than an old man's darling, to young men to avoid old women and marry ugly girls; the "sweetness" of black women; local events such as a cricket match, a grand fire, a white man caught by his wife caressing the black servant, the island riots of 1937; visits of the Graf Zeppelin, royal honeymooners, President Roosevelt; international occurrences such as the abdication of Edward VIII, the Munich settlement, the Italo-Ethiopian War—these are the themes, always amusing, invariably clever, of these local songs. In some of them the addition of a few words in "patois", as a language unknown to the whites, adds to the interest and often to the vulgarity.

Compare, on the other hand, the rich contributions of the Negro in Cuba. Two of Cuba's greatest poets in the slavery era were Plácido, a free mulatto, and Manzano, a Negro slave. By the end of the nineteenth

80

century Brindis de Salas, a famous Negro pianist, had attained a European and American reputation, and was known as "the Black Paganini" and "the king of the octaves". Negroes have made such a contribution to the art of Cuba, as much as the Indian in South America, that Dr. Fernando Ortíz has said that "the Indian in Cuba was the Negro." Today one of Cuba's leading sculptors is the mulatto Rámos Blanco, a former policeman, whose bust of the outstanding colored Cuban general, Antonio Maceo, has recently been acquired by Howard University. Many of Cuba's public monuments have been sculptured by Negroes; one of the most famous, the monument to the mother of the Maceos, in the Mariana Grajales Park, is the work of Rámos Blanco. Another excellent work of this artist is his bust "Cuba", representing the three blood strains of Cuba, white, Negro, and mulatto. At the art school of San Alejandro, out of a faculty of twenty-six, four are Negroes, one of them being Rámos Blanco. An honor student of that school, Caridad Ramírez Medina, is today curator of the works of art in Cuba's Capitol. The two most distinguished poets in Cuba today are Nicholas Guillén, a mulatto, one of whose collections, "West Indies Ltd", shows a Caribbean consciousness rare in the particularism of the area; and Regino Pedroso, a mixture of Asiatic and white. The well-known soprano, Zoila Gálvez, called the "Marian Anderson of Cuba", is a mulatto. Two years ago the mulatto painter, Alberto Peña, familiarly known as Peñita, died, leaving a gap not only in the artistic life of Cuba, but in that of Latin America. His work was the work of a rebel, his themes the economic, political and social life of Cuba. After Price Mars, the eminent sociologist, one of Haiti's foremost men of letters is Jacques Roumain. Afro-Antillean poetry in Puerto Rico is represented by Luis Pales Matos.

81

What is the reason for the overwhelming superiority of Cuba? A partial explanation is probably to be found in the relative independence of Cuba, particularly since 1898. That is not the whole answer, if we consider that Cuba was a Spanish colony up to 1898. But even under Spanish rule there was a distinct Cuban nationality, in fact if not in law. If the Spanish heritage has not entirely disappeared, at least political emancipation made it possible for a national art, a national literature to arise, drawing from the soil in which it sprung. There is no distinct nationality in the British or French islands, only a parasitic clinging to the Old World and Old World ideas which have no place in the New or in communities of different origin and different economic foundation. As elsewhere in the world, a native art, a native literature can arise only when the dead hand of alien control is removed. When that time comes, the Negro will, as elsewhere, play his part in that rebirth.

82

CHAPTER VIII

THE POLITICAL PROBLEM

With the transportation of the Negro from Africa to the Caribbean the germ of political revolt was transplanted to the New World. Contrary to the belief widely accepted among both whites and Negroes, the Negro slave was not docile and devoted to his master. The moment he was placed on the small tubs which made the Middle Passage, that moment he became a revolutionary, actual or potential. His first thought on reaching the islands was to run away to the woods. He became the "cimarrón" of Cuba, the "maroon" of Jamaica, the "bush Negro" of Guiana. No bloodhounds, no posses could hunt him out and the existence of the runaways had to be recognized by the island governments, leaving a standing example to the less fortunate slaves, who resorted to suicide, abortions, poison, murder, anything to cheat the slave-owner. White historians have never been able to understand this. The planter might think the state of slavery eternal, ordained by God, fortified by scriptural precepts, but why should the slave think the same? Slavery was a state of war, a constant struggle for freedom on the part of the slave. Liberty or death! We have a Patrick Henry in America, a Toussaint L'ouverture in Haiti. To the Negro, least of all races in the world, was this a meaningless platitude.

A correct idea of the revolutionary role of the Negro slave is necessary to an appreciation of the political activity of the Negro freeman. As in the United States, the Negro slave in the Caribbean fought for his freedom. As early as 1503 there was a slave rebellion in Cuba. The great slave revolt in French Saint Domingue, the great slave leaders L'ouverture, Dessalines, Christophe, are only one episode in the chapter of Negro slave revolutions. The revolt of Aponte in 1812, the conspiracy of 1844 in which the poet Plácido was framed and shot, made Cuban slaveowners apprehensive of a Cuban Saint Domingue. In 1833 the slaveowner in the British colonies was "sitting, dirty and begrimed, over a powder magazine, from which he would not go away, and he was hourly afraid that the slave would apply a torch to it." The French decree of 1848 abolishing Negro slavery found that institution already abolished in the French colonies by independent action of the governors in the face of the threatening attitude of the slaves. The Cuban slaveowners, fighting the mother country for independence, could not afford the military danger of sabotage from the slaves. The slaves were freed on condition that they joined the revolutionary armies, and the achievements of Antonio Maceo, the high rank he held in the Cuban armies, testify to the blows struck by the Negro in his own and the island's emancipation.

The abolition of Negro slavery left economic and political power in the hands of the former slaveowners. Unlike the United States, there was no Reconstruction. The political activity of the Negroes after emancipation centered on the destruction of the power of the white oligarchy. It was a two-sided struggle. On the part of the middle class it was a struggle for a share in political power, for extension of the franchise, for jobs. On the part of the working class it was basically an economic struggle, a struggle for land ownership, for better wages, for decent living conditions, for the right to organize in trade unions. Sometimes the two movements would coalesce. In 1865 a rebellion took place in Jamaica urging the extension of land settlement and political power: out of a total population of 440,000 only 1900 had the right to vote. The slogan was raised: "Jamaica for the black man!" Coming two years after emancipation in the United States, the whites were in panic. The rebellion was suppressed with the bloodiest cruelty with the aid of the Maroons. Under the infamous Governor Eyre, over four hundred were shot, one thousand Negro houses were burnt, children's brains were dashed out, pregnant women ripped open. What a Royal Commission described as "reckless and positively barbarous" floggings were administered to thousands, sometimes two hundred lashes each, with a cat-o'-nine tails in the strings of which piano wire was interwoven. The white aristocracy, fearful of the growing power of the colored middle class who were beginning to qualify for the franchise, themselves begged the home government to be relieved of their self-governing status and to be reduced to the rank of a crown colony, that is, subject to legislation by the British Parliament. The Water Riots of 1903 in Trinidad, which saw a mass revolt in Port-of-Spain with the working class tearing up the paving stones, ended in the appointment of two colored middle class men to positions in the bureaucracy. But on the whole the two movements, middle class and working class have remained clearly distinct. Up to 1935 the middle class occupied the center of the stage; since 1935 the working class have forged ahead, and today the colored middle class have to choose, it would seem, between the white aristocracy on the one hand and the resurgent black masses on the other.

Let us consider more closely the nature of these two political movements. First, the middle class movement.

Juan Gualberto Gómez was the greatest political leader of color in the history of Cuba. Born on a sugar plantation in Matanzas in 1854, he died in 1933, a Senator of the Republic, one of Cuba's great men. He was fourteen when Céspedes raised the standard of rebellion against Spain and freed his slaves. Gómez, from that day, devoted himself to his double task, the freedom of Cuba and the redemption of the Negro. Throughout his career he remained a Cuban first and a Negro second. Founder of a newspaper "Fraternity", his whole life was a repetition of the theme that the indispensable basis of Cuban nationhood was the union of whites and Negroes. Cuba, he always insisted, was not Haiti. In the French colony the non-whites had outnumbered the whites 24:1, in the Spanish colony the whites outnumbered the non-whites 2:1. The Cuban slaves could therefore harbor no designs of vengeance. Gómez, harping on this theme, played no mean role in the chain of conspiratorial events which resulted in the independence of Cuba. He was a close friend of Martí and other revolutionary leaders. Jailed repeatedly for sedition and separatism, he was elected a member of the revolutionary assembly and representative in the Constituent Assembly, and this great colored champion of the independence of Cuba from Spain was one of the leaders of the "anti-plattistas" or opponents of the Platt Amendment imposed by the United States. It was Gómez who was selected in 1901 to express the views of a special parliamentary commission on the Platt Amendment. Accepting the conditions that Cuba should sign no treaty or contract no debts with foreign powers other than the United States, he resolutely opposed the clause giving the United States the right of intervention in Cuban affairs. It would be to give up the key to Cuba's house, it would make the Cuban statesmen the docile instruments of a foreign and irresponsible power. The demand for naval and coaling stations could not

86

be granted. The terms of the United States Government were harsh, onerous and humiliating, a limitation of Cuba's independence and sovereignty. Had the United States fought and defeated Spain or Cuba?[1]

This was not a Negro speaking, it was a Cuban. It was the language of a Cuban patriot who had studied in Paris and travelled in Mexico. It was the language of a Cuban champion who would be given the Grand Cross of Cárlos Manuel de Céspedes for his services to Cuba. It was the language of a man who, in a Latin environment, was first a man and only incidentally a man of color. Where Frederick Douglass was the voice of the Negro, Gualberto Gómez was the voice of the Cuban. In the United States there were Negroes who were nationalists, in the Caribbean there were nationalists who were Negroes.

What Juan Gualberto Gómez was to Cuba, José Celso Barbosa was to Puerto Rico, an eminent colored middle class leader, voicing the aspirations not of his race but of his compatriots of all races in a period of transition and adjustment. Born in 1857, Barbosa died in 1921; like Gómez respected and honored by all, irrespective of race or color. His grandfather had received a Cross of Merit for his bravery in suppressing a slave rising on a large plantation in Toa Baja, and throughout his long career the grandson was to prove himself a Puerto Rican, and only incidentally a colored Puerto Rican. Like Gómez an ardent supporter of separatism from Spain, Barbosa differed from the Cuban in his attitude to the new power in the Caribbean, the United States. The two most famous men in Puerto Rico in 1897 were Muñoz Rivera, white, and José Barbosa, colored. The one founded the Federal Party, the other the Republican Party. An American, white or Negro, would be tempted to assume that Barbosa was the champion of the Negro

87

minority and Rivera the champion of the white majority. There was essentially no difference between the two party leaders, except this: they both were opposed to the perpetuation of Puerto Rico's colonial status, they both wanted statehood (Puerto Rico's incorporation into the new mother country as the forty-ninth state), but whereas Rivera favored complete independence if the demand for statehood was refused, Barbosa wanted statehood, the whole of statehood, and nothing but statehood. He was opposed to the creation of an independent republic on the Cuban pattern. Nominated member of the island's Executive Council five consecutive times by Presidents of different parties in the United States, Barbosa spoke for Puerto Rico. He opposed plantations of more than five hundred acres, he favored the use of English in the schools as the official language. There was nothing specifically concerning the Negro in his political activity, except an attempt to get scholarships for students of color to the United States, where he himself had studied. Honored by his alma mater, Michigan, with an honorary Master of Arts in 1903 and by the University of Puerto Rico with an honorary Doctor of Laws in 1917, Barbosa was an excellent Puerto Rican, a prominent and well-loved citizen, whose name has been commemorated by one of the streets of San Juan. Like Gómez he was a Negro by the accident of birth.[2]

What has been said of Cuba and Puerto Rico is broadly true of the other areas. In Haiti the issue is clear. The middle classes are the government, European in outlook, gradually becoming American. The career of Ulisses Heureaux, one-time President of the Dominican Republic, is an example of mulatto prestige in that republic. Before the Vichy regime French islands enjoyed a large measure of autonomy. They were dominated by the middle class, and with the privilege of sending one senator and two deputies each to the parliament in Paris, a Candace or a Lémery was given an opportunity to hold forth on a larger stage and in front of a larger audience. The British West Indies, especially since 1918, saw an increasingly vociferous demand on the part of the middle classes for racial equality in the civil service, democratic institutions, widening of the franchise, constitutional reform and federation of the islands. Representative associations sprang up throughout the islands. As a result of this agitation the Colonial Office sent Major Wood (now Lord Halifax) to visit the colonies in 1921. Major Wood opposed the idea of federation, recommended the introduction of a minority of middle class elected members into the Legislative Councils on a restricted basis (as seen above), and gave the British Government a warning which it is not inappropriate to recall today: "The whole history of the African population of the West Indies inevitably drives them towards representative institutions fashioned after the British model. . . .We shall be wise if we avoid the mistake of endeavoring to withhold a concession ultimately inevitable until it has been robbed by delay of most of its usefulness and of all its grace."[3]

The concessions recommended in the Wood Report failed to satisfy the rising consciousness of the colored class. In addition the tendency in the Caribbean was to put the clock back rather than forward. The elected members, colored, of the Legislative Council in British Guiana had control of the purse. As far back as 1907 an absentee investor spoke as follows about this situation: "I do not believe that in any colony of the Empire the white element should be subject to the coloured, whether it be black, brown, or yellow—African, East Indian, or Mongolian."[4] From that time up to 1927 a vigorous campaign was waged against

89

this system as not conducive to sound financial policy and as vesting power in the hands of a group permanently divorced, under the Crown Colony system, from responsibility. In 1928 Guiana was brought in line with the other established colonies. The Governor was given control of the purse, and the elected members were swamped by a host of nominated members introduced to secure an official majority.[5] A local Commission, appointed in 1934 to study the question of the franchise, refused to recommend the lowering of the income qualification and even inclined to raising the standard in the hope that this would secure "a purer electorate".[6]

It was in the midst of the dissatisfaction in the islands that the British Government announced in 1932 a Commission to consider the possibility of closer union between Trinidad and the Windward and Leeward Islands. Immediately a West Indian Conference was called in Dominica in November 1932 to elaborate a Constitution based on federation and full elective control of the legislative assemblies. Enthusiasm was great in the islands. The middle class associations had no program specifically in the interest of the working class, though the Trinidad and Grenada groups (significantly called Workingmen's Associations) advocated slum clearance and workmen's compensation. Yet this liberal, narrowly middle class program attracted widespread mass support. The Dominica Conference foundered on the rock of the franchise. No agreement could be reached on the question of adult suffrage, and the compromise adopted, permitting each colony to settle its own franchise qualifications, showed clearly the unsympathetic attitude of the colored middle class to the aspirations of the barefooted man. The Commission itself opposed the idea of federation, endorsed the system of nomination of some councillors, and was

90

emphatic in its opposition to "the grant of universal adult suffrage until the present standard of education in the islands has greatly advanced."[7] The Negro is deliberately denied education, and then his illiteracy is used as an argument against the grant of the franchise. As if education precedes democracy, instead of following it! But the middle class capitulation was complete. A government job for one of the radical leaders, a dinner appointment with the governor for another, an invitation to a party at Buckingham Palace for a third, and the radicals vanished into thin air. White aristocracy or black masses—the intermediate colored middle class had chosen. The stage was set for the barefooted man.

The events of the years 1935–1938 mark a revolution in the history of the British Caribbean islands. The initiative passed from the brown middle class to the black working class. Rawle, Marryshow and Cipriani (a white liberal), gave way to Butler and Bustamente, Payne and Grant. It is no longer the aspirations of the middle class, but the demands of the working class, that are being discussed. Industrial legislation, slum clearance, social services, compensation for agricultural workers and domestic servants, land settlement—these are the questions of the present and the future. These issues started that train of revolt which spread from island to island and attracted world-wide attention to the problems of the Caribbean Negro.

At various periods before 1935 there had been labor unrest in the British West Indies and attempts at the formation of Workingmen's Associations. It is significant that one of the most important of these uprisings took place in Trinidad in 1919 during the international unrest which followed the World War. There was a general strike of the dock workers in Port-of-Spain, the capital. The workers took control of the town, and the chief of police admitted later at an inquiry that he could not trust his black policemen to shoot on the black masses. During this period of international crisis, and for a year or two after, a not very unimportant part was played by the Garvey movement in the United States. The relation between Garvey's United Negro Improvement Association and the British West Indies is of importance both for what it did not achieve and for what it actually did, as well as for its significance for recent political developments in the islands.

Garvey and his wife were Jamaicans by birth. Active, anxious to take political action, significantly they did so not in Jamaica but in the United States, where they felt that, in contrast to Jamaica, political activity could be carried on. They both were people of great energy and ability, and they used the upheaval in world society after the war and the large-scale migration of Negroes from the South to the North as a basis for a tremendous mass movement. Garvey recruited many of his lieutenants from the West Indies, people who, one may presume, would naturally have been political leaders in the islands had they found sufficient scope there. What is remarkable, however, is that as the movement grew in the United States, it had serious repercussions in the West Indies, and, in the days when the movement was at its height, Garvey's paper was widely sold in the islands. The government of Trinidad banned it, which did not prevent its active circulation. Groups of Garveyites were formed who sent money and followed the history of the movement closely. The islands were represented by delegations at conventions of the U.N.I.A.

While there was not much to be seen in the islands in the way of concrete organization, it is unquestionable that the Garvey Movement in the United States exercised an extraordinary stimulating effect upon Negro race consciousness among the poorer classes of the British West Indies. For Garvey's appeal was not so much to the Negro in general as to the man with a black skin in particular. The influence he exercised was almost exclusively confined to the masses, and the West Indian middle classes were, almost without exception, viciously hostile. Had a movement of the Garvey type existed in the United States during 1932 or 1933, during the depression, it would have had incalculable effects upon the recent movements in the West Indies, not only as a political stimulus but as a factor in their concrete organization.

Consider the chronology of these fateful years 1935–1938. A sugar strike in St. Kitts, 1935; a revolt against increase of customs duties in St. Vincent, 1935; a coal strike in St. Lucia, 1935; labor disputes on the sugar plantations of British Guiana, 1935; an oil strike, which became a general strike, in Trinidad, 1937; a sympathetic strike in Barbados, 1937; revolt on the sugar plantations in British Guiana, 1937; a sugar strike in St. Lucia, 1937; sugar troubles in Jamaica, 1937; dockers' strike in Jamaica, 1938. Every governor called for warships, marines and aeroplanes. The torch had been applied to the powder barrel. Total casualties amounted to 29 dead, 115 wounded.

The "agitators" and "hooligans", as they were called, were men of the people. Uriah Butler, the leader in Trinidad, uneducated, with a queer political concoction of God, Marx and the British Empire, yet withal a man of great sincerity, was an ex-serviceman, discriminated against in the first World War, exploited on the Trinidad oilfields. The calypso "Murder at Fyzabad" expressed public feeling in referring to him as "the Great Butler", and public opinion in the island identified the trial scene of Emile Zola in the film currently being shown with Butler's trial. In an island in which 90 per cent of the people are poverty-stricken, a reward of $500 was offered for Butler's arrest. Butler remained in hiding in Port-of-Spain and Venezuela, and no one turned informer. His arrest was due to his decision to give evidence before the Commission sent out from England, on a promise of safe conduct which the police, as usual, did not keep. Payne, Butler's friend, leader in Barbados, was sprung from the masses. Bustamente, the rich labor leader and demagogue, is the idol of Jamaica.

The reason for the widespread revolt was clearly the condition of the people described in an earlier chapter. At the same time the masses had no constitutional means of ventilating their grievances. The strike was a crime, the trade union an unlawful association. One of the most significant results of the revolt has been the increased impetus to unionism. The Bustamente unions in Jamaica claim a membership of 50,000. The Maritime Workers' Union includes well over 90 per cent of the dock workers and seamen in the island. The Oilworkers' Trade Union in Trinidad has over 8,000 members in an industry employing 9,000, and its power in the oil fields is unquestionable. Unions have sprung up in St. Lucia, British Guiana, Barbados, St. Vincent, among rural and urban workers. Labor papers are published everywhere—the *Guiana Review* in British Guiana; the *Barbados Observer; Public Opinion* in Jamaica; the *Pilot,* the *Socialist* and the *People* in Trinidad. New parties have sprung up, with, significantly, some middle class leaders who have not gone the other way. The Progressive League was founded in Barbados. In September 1938 a colored man, Jamaica's leading barrister, Norman Manley, King's Counsel, launched the People's National Party at a meeting at which the late British Ambassador to Russia, Sir Stafford Cripps, was present. The Manpower and Citizen's Association was formed in British Guiana in 1936. There is current talk of forming a People's Party in Trinidad.

The program of these associations, parties and newspapers is Labor. Land settlement, adult suffrage, social legislation, trade union organization, full democracy—these are their demands. Negro and Indian, with a portion of the mulatto element, are collaborating. The most respected trade union leader in Trinidad is Rienzi, an Indian. The climax of this new development was reached in November 1938 when a Labor Congress of the West Indies and British Guiana met in British Guiana. The demands included: federation; a purely elected legislature, elected by universal suffrage, with regards to which the governor is to have the power of the King of England in relation to the Parliament; nationalization of the sugar industry; prohibition of plantations larger than fifty acres; co-operative marketing; state ownership of public utilities; social legislation such as old age pensions, national health insurance, unemployment insurance, minimum wage, 44-hour week, workmen's compensation and trade union immunities; free compulsory elementary education.

In the words of a West Indian student: "The Labour Movement is on the march. It has already behind it a history of great achievement in a short space of time. It will make of the West Indies of the future a country where the common man may lead a cultured life in freedom and prosperity."[8] But the Labor Movement is fighting against powerful obstacles. The great weapon of employers is victimization, and they do not hesitate to use it. Labor leaders are shadowed by the police, the sedition laws are very elastic. A prominent British trade unionist signed the report of the Trinidad Disturbances Commission which denied unions the right of peaceful picketing or protection against action in tort. The British Labor Party has never made it a practice to encourage the affiliation of colonial unions, but unrest in the West Indies reached such a pitch that the British Government was forced to send out a Royal Commission in 1939, with Sir Walter Citrine, Secretary of the Trades Union Congress, as one of its leading members. Local governments exercise the right of withholding registration from unions of which they disapprove. Negroes, refusing to suspend their constitutional struggles during the war, are accused of playing Hitler's game, of fouling democracy's nest. But white employers in the British West Indies are openly gloating over the opportunities provided by the war of regaining the concessions wrung from them and drillers on the Trinidad oilfields are already talking about "what they are going to give the niggers next time".[9] "It is clear", writes an English journal devoted to colonial matters about Trinidad, "that the colonial Government is anxiously seeking to use the war as an excuse for withdrawing the very limited democratic rights that exist and smashing the young Trade Union movement in the West Indies."[10] Every labor leader in the colonies, Bustamente, Payne, Butler, is in gaol under the Emergency Powers Act while labor leaders in England occupy positions in the War Cabinet. A Jamaican, domiciled in the United States, was recently arrested and imprisoned on his return to Jamaica, on the ground that he had been "engaged in defeatist and anti-war propaganda, including propaganda designed to stimulate opposition on racial grounds to the establishment of United States Bases in the West

96

Indies." Sir Leonard Lyle, sugar baron in England, justified the arrest on the ground of the necessity of proscribing "agitation" during the war. But the arrest has provoked such resentment among West Indians at home and abroad that the British Government has sent out a special undersecretary to investigate. The tension is unabated. Public meetings are prohibited. In the face of opposition in Trinidad to the prohibition of the assembling of more than ten persons, the number was increased to twenty. As a labor paper sarcastically wrote, only nineteen could pay attention, for number twenty would have to keep a sharp lookout to prevent any one else from joining the meeting.

Small groups of West Indians abroad, like the League of Colored Peoples and the International African Service Bureau in England, the Jamaica Progressive League in the United States, have been making their voices heard in recent years, however ineffectively. A more recent association is the West Indies National Emergency Committee, an association overriding insular boundaries, established in the United States. The Committee sent a representative to the Havana Conference to present the case for the islands. Their words may be quoted: "The inhabitants in these areas have long since reached that stage in historical evolution where they have demonstrated their capacity for practical administration of government in accordance with modern democratic technique. West Indians participate in every department of government—legislative, executive, judicial—to such an extent that only a few posts are administered by Europeans solely because of the existing imperial connections."[11] They are opposed to what the Argentine delegate at the Havana Conference called "the substitution of one regime of European colonies by another of American colonies," and are demanding for the Negro in the

Caribbean Dominion Status, the Constitution of Canada.

Outside of the British West Indies the Negro masses also are stirring. In Cuba, where they are in a minority, they are the object of special concern of the Cuban Confederation of Labor, affiliated to the Third International. This labor organization is exceptionally strong in the sugar industry, where the Negroes predominate. Their demands for an 8-hour day and for 80 per cent Cuban employees are in the interest of the Cuban Negro who is undercut by his fellow Negroes from Haiti or Jamaica. The Confederation of Labor has a special Secretary for Negro affairs and special departments dealing with Negro matters. In their specific appeal to the Negro wage-earner, they demand equal wages with white workers, the abolition of all racial discrimination, and the adoption of the principle that in all hiring contracts one-half of the employees must be Negro. In the elections held in 1940 in Cuba there were colored candidates who ran on the Communist Party ticket.

Puerto Rico has travelled far since the days of Barbosa and his program of statehood. A new party has arisen, the Nationalist Party, demanding complete and unconditional independence, but there is no indication that any special appeal is being made to the Negro as a group. If the observations of a Spanish writer are to be trusted, the Negroes are sympathetic to the United States.[12] The undiluted dictatorship in the Dominican Republic presses on all colors alike. With humanity at the crossroads, there are, for the Caribbean as for the rest of the world, for the Negro as for the rest of mankind, only two alternatives: greater freedom or greater tyranny.

CHAPTER IX

THE FUTURE OF THE CARIBBEAN

We have described the many ills in the Pandora's box of foreign domination. The reader is now in a position to consider the changes that are imperative. The future of the Caribbean is partly an internal and partly an external problem. In the one case the inhabitants can contribute to the solution of their own problems; in the other case they are at the mercy of the forces which are at present operating in the whole world.

Any solution of the internal problem would be meaningless which continues to ignore the extension of full democratic privileges to the Negro. At present the Caribbean lives under a government of sugar, for sugar, by sugar. Under such a government revenues come less from direct taxation of land, industry and incomes, than from indirect taxation which falls chiefly on imports, that is, the food of the masses. For the whole British West Indian area 40 per cent of the revenue comes from import duties, only five per cent from income taxes. The corresponding figures for the mother country show 24 and 35 per cent respectively.[1] Sugar employers oppose the 8-hour day. The representative of the Sugar Manufacturers' Association in Trinidad in 1926 gave it as "the considered opinion of every sugar manufacturer in the Island that there is nothing to be gained by an 8-hour day, and, further, the employers and employees would not like it."[2] In 1937 the Government of Trinidad thought a minimum wage an "unwise venture"[3]—like that unofficial member in British Nyasaland nominated by the government from the missionaries who thought it unnecessary to substitute a legal for a human relationship between employer and worker.

Governments in the past have consistently intervened on the side of sugar. Tariffs, subsidies, concessions of all kinds have been made whenever the planters mentioned the first word in their vocabulary, "ruin"—a word invariably used to designate "not the poverty of the people, not the want of food or raiment, not even the absence of riches or luxury, but simply the decrease of sugar cultivation." Governments must now intervene on the side of labor. If history teaches us any lessons, it teaches us that it is only in the democratic solution that the conflict of interests can be resolved. Full and unqualified democracy—nothing less. The true Magna Carta of these colonies is economic emancipation, but the road to economic emancipation demands political democracy. The words of a white resident of Trinidad in 1889 in favor of self-government are still pertinent today: "I am sorry to say we have had some very ricketty people as officials here sent out from home. . . .Up to this time we have been nursed in the arms of the Colonial Office. . . .We have never been put down to creep, leaving out of the question to try to walk."[4]

What are the alternatives to political democracy? The islands can, in the first place, stay as they are, with a concession here and a concession there. The British Royal Commission of 1939 could only recommend an increase in the sugar export quota of 20 per cent, "to avert the under-employment of plant and labour."[5] More Negroes are to be paid twenty-five cents a day, while the dividends of shareholders must not be diminished. The governor of Jamaica pours scorn on the "prentice hands" with an "itch to govern".

100

Adult suffrage is to be conceded to Jamaica, elected representatives will have a majority over nominated members on the Legislative Council, but the governor is given an over-riding veto. No wonder Jamaica has rejected the "reforms". British Guiana, too, will have a reformed constitution, with a majority of elected representatives who will not be associated with the work of government, with the governor retaining his over-riding powers, and a franchise commission to investigate the possibility of adult suffrage. A commission has been set up in Trinidad to examine the possibilities of widening the franchise—after a trial period lasting until 1948! It was in 1897 that a Royal Commission reported: "We have placed the labouring population of the West Indies where it is and cannot divest ourselves of responsibility for its future." Today, after more than forty years, the Colonial Secretary can still refer to the colonies as "neglected estates", and can only promise fair words. "The British Empire is not to be deflected from its civilising mission, even by the greatest war in history." But where the Royal Commission asked for five million dollars a year for the West Indies, the appropriation for 1941 is $80,000—barely adequate for the salaries of the newly appointed Comptroller of Development and his staff. If British colonials in the West Indies placed hopes in the Atlantic Charter with its self-determination, or were impressed by Deputy Prime Minister Attlee's insistence before an African audience that the right of *all* peoples to choose their form of government meant all peoples, they were soon disillusioned. "At the Atlantic meeting", declared Mr. Churchill, "we had in mind primarily restoration of the sovereignty, self-government and national life of the States and nations of Europe. . . .That is quite a separate problem from the progressive evolution

101

of self-governing institutions in the regions and peoples which owe allegiance to the British Crown."

The islands can, in the second place, be traded for war debts or more destroyers, or simply taken over by the United States. The solution of the Cuban sugar problem, it is argued, is that Cuba should become an American colony, within the American tariff walls. Must the United States, then, take over all these colonies which produce sugar that she cannot consume? It will be interesting to see the reaction of the sugar interests of the United States and its present territories to such a policy. Or will she take over the colonies for the mere pleasure of governing more Negroes?

The Negro's right to decide his own affairs and his own life is not a question for argument. His opinions were never considered on so important a question as the granting of bases to a foreign power. Eire has not yet been persuaded into giving bases to the mother country. A Canadian member of the British Parliament, speaking on this issue said: "At such a moment we are not going to say to Americans, 'wait a minute, the Parliament of Great Britain wants to talk about terms and colour ban and nigger problems.'" This was not the German Reichstag, it was the British Parliament. Not a single protest was made against this contemptuous epithet. That is the fascist mentality and democracy today cannot afford to be tainted with a fascist limitation.

There is no cause, moreover, to fear the Negroes. They are not traitors, nor are they fifth columnists. The British West Indies contributed 15,601 officers and men, large donations in cash, numerous gifts of food, to the British War effort in 1914–1918. Today they are contributing pilots and squadrons of planes. There has always been treason in the Caribbean, never

102

among the Negroes. At the first mention of abolition of the slave trade in England, a British merchant, John Pinney, sugar planter in Nevis, thought of the British colonies "under the dominion of some wiser European power". The fear that France would abolish the slave trade drove Saint Domingue and the other colonies to offer themselves to England. "What right has the King of England to Jamaica except that he stole it from Spain?" asked a Jamaican planter in 1831, apprehensive of emancipation, and the planters were talking of annexation by the United States. Jamaica and British Guiana in the forties refused to grant supplies and their constitutions had to be suspended. Some Spanish planters in Cuba and Puerto Rico openly encouraged and supported the annexationist designs of the slaveowners of the United States. Whatever fifth columnists and traitors there are over the Caribbean today must be sought among the white ruling classes, British, French and Spanish, not among the Negro masses.

Only popular governments in the British colonies could hope to introduce that political federation which is called for not only by economic considerations but by every dictate of common sense. Imagine nineteen scattered units, each with its own complicated governmental structure, customs service, medical system, police, etc., each run at enormous expense. No one need argue today the value of one single expert agricultural service for all the islands. It is not the sea which has stood in the way of federation, but the opposition of local potentates, big bosses over small areas. As Major Wood wrote in 1921: "the principal opponents of a change were the Trinidad Chamber of Commerce, who represent the leading merchants of the colony, and who are a body whose views deserve to carry weight. They regard the demand as inspired

103

by movements largely external to the colony, and pointed to the prosperity of Trinidad under its existing form of government."[6] The aeroplane has linked up the islands. The federation of the administrative services, reducing the number of governors and bureaucrats, followed by the establishment of a federal legislature, is essential to future progress. The chairman of the Royal Commission of 1939 has stated that he "could not look to any uniform system of government in the component parts" of the British West Indies.[7] But that is the old order, and it seems destined to go.

Not only a political federation of the various units according to nationality, but an economic federation of all the Caribbean areas is the path of statesmanship in the future. It is reported that a plan, drafted by Administration experts in the United States, has been submitted to President Roosevelt urging Anglo-American collaboration "to solve the economic ills of the millions of Latins (sic) living in Cuba, Haiti, Jamaica, the Dominican Republic, Puerto Rico and the Virgin Islands."[8] But the problem is Caribbean in scope. These islands have a common heritage of slavery, a labor base essentially the same. Burdened by the same curse, sugar, the dynamics of the different areas are the same, and it is time to pay more heed to the fundamental identities than to the incidental differences. Too long has man been allowed to triumph over nature and geographical unity has too long been sacrificed to political and artificial divisions. An economic federation of all the areas will considerably strengthen their bargaining position in the world market. It would take a federation of democratic governments to settle the burning land question and introduce that program of diversification so necessary to a sound and healthy economic structure. If it be objected that the federation visualized is impracticable, it may be answered

104

that the Caribbean, like the whole world, will federate or collapse.

Progressive opinion in the Caribbean today is looking inquiringly towards the Haitian example. That country points a moral which well deserves to be studied and heeded. If Haiti is the standing example of how the Negro can be driven to desperation, it is also the standing example of how a successful political revolution can be frustrated in some of its potentialities for progress by conservative economic practises. Haiti's wealth was sugar. Their revolution destroyed that wealth. Economic progress, political reform and social security cannot be achieved by destructive means. Sugar is the curse, but it is also the staple, of the Caribbean. The explosions in the British West Indies indicate the danger of continued exasperation and continued repression; there is still time to heed the signals and so correct, by democratic reforms, an unsound economy and the present abuses of the sugar industry.

So much for the internal aspect of the solution. These democratic areas, federated politically or economically, will be ready and willing to take their part and fulfill the obligations imposed on them by membership in the Pan-American Federation. But political democracy by itself is no solution of their problem. The West Indian islands are entirely dependent on the world market. Their fate is bound up with the fate of the world market. The islands have for three centuries paid a high price for their monoculture and industrial backwardness; the "dance of the millions" in years of prosperity, misery and bankruptcy in years of over-production. Their future hinges not only upon the establishment of a diversified production in the islands rendering them independent of imported food, but also of a rational economy in the world, in which commodities will be produced in areas to which they are best suited, and in which the proposals of nature will not be flouted by man's ersatz and sacrificed to political considerations of autarchy. Until that blessed day dawns, their strategic situation is going to insist that the economic current of the islands flows in the same direction—the direction of the Western Hemisphere.

The Caribbean, in fact, is geographically and economically an American lake. It was in recognition of this fact that shrewd observers of American Independence declared that Britain had lost not only thirteen colonies but eight islands as well. Historic American attempts to acquire Cuba, by fair means or foul, to secure naval bases in Haiti and the Dominican Republic, together with the acquisition of Puerto Rico by conquest and the Virgin Islands by purchase, are so many milestones on the road of a domination that in many respects is a natural one. Equally natural is the economic domination, hampered, however by the political affiliations of the islands. The French islands have always been supplied by and suppliers of the home market. The Ottawa Agreements of the British Empire diverted British West Indian trade from its normal channels. In 1930, 26 per cent of British West Indian exports went to the United States; in 1933, only 7 per cent. Total United States exports to the British West Indies declined by more than half, comparing the averages for the decades 1926–1930 and 1931–1935, though by 1938 they had risen a further 75 per cent. Similarly United States imports from the British West Indies declined by nearly two-thirds in the same period, and fell a further 45 per cent by 1938.

But the Ottawa Agreements are not the whole explanation. United States imports have fallen more drastically than exports. The imports are tropical produce, which the United States gets from other sources; the exports are chiefly machinery, which the United States, if only because of its location, can supply more cheaply than any other competitor. If the Ottawa Agreements were the British aspect of the Anglo-American tariff war, the Hawley-Smoot Tariff was the American. Under this tariff United States exports to Cuba declined by two-thirds comparing the decades 1926–1930 and 1931–1935, imports from Cuba by more than three-fifths. Exports to the Dominican Republic declined by more than three-fifths, imports more than half; exports to Haiti by more than three-fifths, imports by one-third.[9] The United States dominates these islands completely, it can make or break them. They cannot be politically and strategically a part of the New World and economically a part of the Old. The United States cannot be a military friend and an economic enemy of the Caribbean. The burdens of hemisphere defence must be equitably distributed and the American farmer made to bear his share.

Some scheme, if the good neighbor policy is to survive, will have to be devised by which surpluses that normally went to Europe will be consumed in the Western Hemisphere. In recommending to Congress the arrangement by which leases on the bases were conceded to the United States, President Roosevelt described it as "the most important action in the reinforcement of our national defense that has been taken since the Louisiana Purchase." So important a transaction must mean more to the islands than steel and reinforced concrete and swamp reclamation for bases. The United States' tariff policy ruined Cuba in the interest of the cane growers of Louisiana and the beet farmers of Colorado. Problems of hemisphere defence are mutual, not unilateral, and the islands need defence not only against Hitler but also against starvation and excruciating poverty. British trusteeship has become the Dual Mandate and the United States cannot evade its responsibilities. Puerto Rico was solemnly promised, in 1898, the blessings of good government. Instead it got the curses of sugar. If the new responsibilities of the United States are restricted to sugar plantations and racial discrimination, the future of America's new wards is hopeless indeed. It is far more than a question of introducing to softball backward natives whose national pastime is cricket or changing a left-hand to a right-hand drive. The Havana Conference of 1940 called for a raising of the standard of living in the Caribbean territories. "There ought to be", in the words of an American student, "some better way of doing it than turning loose a lot of private corporations to make all the money they can for their stockholders."[10]

There are endless possibilities for the increase of consumption in the American republics, above all in the islands themselves. This is a matter calling for knowledge of experts who will not think themselves obliged to justify the status quo and whitewash the sugar planter. Such expert knowledge is not within the capacity of the writer, but it is suggested that no permanent solution can be found for the future welfare of the Caribbean which does not have as its aim and purpose the raising of the standard of living in the area, and so raise the productive capacity of the islands, at present limited by international agreements. This is the contribution that the United States can make. It is widely rumored that, at the insistence of the British Government, the American authorities have refused to pay wages in the new bases above the current level, while public feeling in the islands has been antagonized by American refusal to negotiate with

108

the trade unions. Yet both America and Britain are at home supposed to be giving every encouragement to collective bargaining. The United States must accept economic responsibility for an area to whose protection it is committed and for whose miseries it is in part to blame. That, or the alternative—Yankee imperialism and the almighty dollar. "The real 'yankee peril' ", as Dr. Knight wrote of the Dominican Republic, "is the process of economically North-Americanizing the western hemisphere. . . .There is a danger that we may take the prosperity and leave . . . the posterity—a horde of laborers to make sugar for the coffee cups of the Temperate Zone."[11]

REFERENCE NOTES

CHAPTER III

[1] *The Foreign Trade of Latin America*, Part II. (United States Tariff Commission, Washington, D. C., 1940). Sections on Cuba, Haiti, Dominican Republic.

[2] Percentages estimated from *Anuario Azucarero de Cuba, 1940* (Habana, 1940), from tables for the different provinces for 1939.

[3] *Report of the Royal Franchise Commission* (Port-of-Spain, 1889), Sixteenth Meeting, p. 22. Evidence of Mr. R. Guppy, July 14, 1888.

[4] W. A. Beckles: *The Barbados Disturbances, 1937* (Bridgetown, 1937), p. 245.

[5] *Health and Socio-Economic Studies in Puerto Rico: On a Sugar Cane Plantation* (San Juan, 1937), p. 63.

[6] *Rehabilitation in Puerto Rico* (Puerto Rico, 1939).

[7] *Health and Socio-Economic Conditions in the Tobacco, Coffee and Fruit Regions* ("Puerto Rico Journal of Public Health and Tropical Medicine," March 1939), p. 261.

[8] *The West Indies Today* (London, n. d.), p. 29.

[9] E. B. Hill and S. L. Descartes: *An Economic Background for Agricultural Research in Puerto Rico* (Rio Piedras, 1939), p. 15.

[10] *Health and Socio-Economic Conditions in the Tobacco, Coffee and Fruit Regions*, p. 255.

[11] G. St. J. Orde Browne: *Labour Conditions in the West Indies* (London, 1938), pp. 82, 86.

[12] *Health and Socio-Economic Studies in Puerto Rico: On a Sugar Cane Plantation*, p. 63.

[13] R. Picó: *Puerto Rico: Economic Sore Spot* ("Inter-American Quarterly", April 1940), p. 66.

[14] H. T. Pooley: *The Future of the Caribbean Colonies* ("Empire Production and Export", June 1927), p. 435.

CHAPTER IV

[1] *The Barbados Disturbances, 1937*, pp. 275, 282.

[2] C. C. Rogler: *Comerio, A Study of a Puerto Rican Town* (Kansas, 1940), pp. 52–53.

[3] E. A. Bird: *Report on the Sugar Industry in Relation to the Social and Economic System of Puerto Rico* (San Juan, 1937), p. 91.

[4] *Trinidad and Tobago Disturbances, 1937, Report of Commission*, Cmd. 5641 (His Majesty's Stationery Office, London, 1937), p. 111.

[5] Beckles, *op. cit.*, pp. 244, 250.

[6] Bird, *op. cit.*, p. 43.

[7] *Health and Socio-Economic Studies . . . on a Sugar Cane Plantation*, p. 68.

[8] *Ibid.*, p. 75.

[9] M. Dartigue: *Conditions Rurales en Haiti* (Port-au-Prince, 1938), pp. 6–8.

[10] *Problems of the New Cuba* (New York, 1935), p. 80.

110

[11] *Report of the Nutrition Committee, 1936-1937* (Jamaica, 1937), p. 4.

[12] *Report of the Committee appointed to consider and report on the question of Nutrition in Barbados* (Bridgetown, 1936), p. 5.

[13] *Health and Socio-Economic Studies in Puerto Rico: Physical Measurements of Agricultural Workers*, pp. 454-455, 466.

[14] Cmd. 5641, p. 111.

[15] *Health and Socio-Economic Studies . . . on a Sugar Cane Plantation*, p. 19.

[16] Duke of Montrose, Feb. 23, 1938 (House of Lords).

[17] *Health and Socio-Economic Studies . . . on a Sugar Cane Plantation*, p. 56.

[18] Cmd. 5641, pp. 30-31.

[19] P. M. Otero and M. A. Perez: *Health Work in the Rural Areas of Puerto Rico* ("The Puerto Rico Journal of Public Health and Tropical Medicine", September, 1939), pp. 53-54.

[20] *Health and Socio-Economic Studies . . . on a Sugar Cane Plantation*, p. 12.

[21] *Health Work in the Rural Areas of Puerto Rico*, pp. 61-62.

[22] Harold Stannard in the London "Times", May 25, 1938.

[23] Dartigue, *op. cit*, p. 4.

[24] *Health and Socio-Economic Studies . . . on a Sugar Cane Plantation*, p. 16.

[25] Cmd. 5641, p. 36; R. Cobden: *Trinidad Scene* ("Inside the Empire", May 1940), p. 11.

[26] Quoted by G. Padmore: *England's West Indian Slums* ("Crisis", October 1940), p. 317.

[27] Cmd. 5641, p. 36.

[28] C. F. Andrews: *An Interim Statement Concerning East Indian Conditions in British Guiana* (Georgetown, 1929), p. 23.

[29] Cmd. 5641, pp. 37-38.

[30] *Labour Conditions in the West Indies*, p. 72.

[31] *Health and Socio-Economic Studies . . . on a Sugar Cane Plantation*, p. 13.

[32] *Health and Socio-Economic Conditions in the Tobacco, Coffee and Fruit Regions*, p. 217.

[33] *Health and Socio-Economic Studies, Physical Measurements of Agricultural Workers*, p. 468.

[34] *Health, Sanitation and Vital Statistics on Sugar Estates* (Legislative Council Paper No. 6, 1932, British Guiana), p. 3.

[35] *Survey of the Position as Regards Nutrition in Dominica* (Roseau, 1937), p. 6.

[36] *Health Work in the Rural Areas of Puerto Rico*, p. 59.

[37] *Jamaica Nutrition Committee*, pp. 4, 9.

[38] L. E. Blauch and C. F. Reid: *Public Education in the Territories and Outlying Possessions* (Washington, 1939), pp. 152-153.

[39] *Survey of . . . Nutrition in Dominica*, pp. 5-6.

[40] *Health and Socio-Economic Studies in Puerto Rico: Physical Impairments of Adult Life Among Agricultural Workers* ("The Puerto Rico Journal of Public Health and Tropical Medicine", June 1940), p. 303.

[41] *Jamaica Nutrition Committee*, p. 9.

[42] Dartigue, *op. cit.*, p. 18.

111

43 *Report of the Committee Appointed to Consider . . . Nutrition in Barbados*, p. 7.

44 *Labour Conditions in the West Indies*, p. 78.

45 O. P. Starkey: *The Economic Geography of Barbados* (New York, 1939), p. 183.

46 *Report of the Nutrition Committee in British Guiana* (Georgetown, 1937), p. 25.

47 *Health and Socio-Economic Conditions in the Tobacco, Coffee and Fruit Regions*, p. 225.

48 *Labour Conditions in the West Indies*, p. 28.

49 Information obtained by the writer from a member of the B.M.A.

50 *West Indies Royal Commission, Proceedings of Investigations in Barbados* (Bridgetown, 1939), p. 17.

51 Luis Muñoz Marin. Quoted in B. W. and J. W. Diffie: *Porto Rico: A Broken Pledge* (New York, 1931), p. 45.

CHAPTER V

1 *Proceedings of the Ninth West Indian Agricultural Conference,* (Jamaica, 1925), p. 37.

2 *The Report of the Jamaica Banana Commission, 1936* (Jamaica, 1936), p. 8.

3 Bird, *op. cit.,* p. 75.

4 *Report of the West Indian Sugar Commission*, Part IV, Colonial No. 49 (His Majesty's Stationery Office, 1930), pp. 63–64.

5 R. Picó: *Studies in the Economic Geography of Puerto Rico* (Río Piedras, 1937), p. 49.

6 Bird, *op. cit.,* p. 73.

7 J. B. Delawarde: *La Vie Paysanne à la Martinique* (Fort-de-France, 1937), pp. 62–63.

8 *Report of the West Indian Sugar Commission*, Cmd. 3517 (His Majesty's Stationery Office, 1930), pp. 26, 58.

9 *Report of the Jamaica Unemployment Commission* (Kingston, 1936), Appendix No. XLI, p. 1.

10 Cmd. 5641, p. 45.

11 *Land Settlement and Minimum Wage in St. Vincent* ("Industrial Labour Information", Feb. 15, 1937), pp. 225–226.

12 "Time", Feb. 2, 1942.

13 Bird, *op. cit.,* p. 64.

14 *Problems of the New Cuba,* pp. 51, 271.

15 Cmd. 3517, p. 57.

16 Dartigue, *op. cit.,* p. 10.

17 G. E. Simpson: *Haitian Peasant Economy* ("Journal of Negro History", October 1940), pp. 500–502.

18 *The West Indies Today*, pp. 26–27.

19 *Report of the Small Farmers Committee, 1930* (Legislative Council Paper No. 9 of 1931, British Guiana).

CHAPTER VI

1 Price Mars: *Social Castes and Social Problems in Haiti* ("Inter-American Quarterly", July 1940), p. 79.

2 Sir H. H. Johnston: *The Negro in the New World* (London, 1910), pp. 189–190.

[3] K. Pringle: *Waters of the West* (London, 1938), p. 73.
[4] *Return showing the composition of the local legislatures in the West Indies and in British Guiana* . . . (His Majesty's Stationery Office, 1939), p. 4.
[5] A. Calder-Marshall: *Glory Dead* (London, 1939), p. 64.
[6] C. L. R. James: *The Case for West-Indian Self Government* (London, 1933), pp. 8–9.
[7] Price Mars, *op. cit.*, pp. 78–79.

CHAPTER VII

[1] A. Arredondo: *El Negro en Cuba* (La Habana, 1939), p. 48.
[2] *Report of Select Committee of the Legislative Council on Restriction of Hours of Labour* (Trinidad, 1926), pp. 30–31.
[3] *Ibid.*, p. 32.
[4] *Report of the Economic Investigation Committee* (Georgetown, 1930), pp. 16–17.
[5] *Report of a Commission appointed to consider problems of Secondary and Primary Education in Trinidad, Barbados, Leeward Islands and Windward Islands, 1931–1932* (His Majesty's Stationery Office, 1933), p. 51.
[6] *Problems of the New Cuba*, pp. 134–135, 140, 157.
[7] Blauch and Reid, *op. cit.*, pp. 111, 117; *Report of the Commissioner of Education*, 1931–1934, p. 111; *ibid.*, 1937–1938, p. 44.
[8] Dartigue, *op. cit.*, pp. 24, 27.
[9] *Problems of the New Cuba*, pp. 154–155.

CHAPTER VIII

[1] A biography of Gómez has been published by the Club Atenas of Havana: *Juan Gualberto Gómez, su labor patriótica y sociologia*, vol. 1 (La Habana, 1934).
[2] Documents for the life of Barbosa have been collected and edited by his daughter, Doña Pilar Barbosa de Rosario, in four volumes: *La Obra de José Celso Barbosa* (San Juan, 1937–1939).
[3] *Report by the Hon. E. F. L. Wood, M.P. on his visit to the West Indies and British Guiana*, Cmd. 1679 (His Majesty's Stationery Office, 1922), pp. 6–7.
[4] Sir Edward R. Davson: *British Guiana and its Development* (Paper read before the Royal Colonial Institute, March, 1908), p. 16.
[5] *Report of the British Guiana Commission, 1927*, Cmd. 2841 (His Majesty's Stationery Office, 1927).
[6] *Report of the British Guiana Franchise Commission* (Georgetown, 1935), p. 7.
[7] *West Indies, Report of the Closer Union Commission, 1933*, Cmd. 4383 (His Majesty's Stationery Office, 1933), pp. 7, 17, 21.
[8] W. A. Lewis: *Labour in the West Indies* (London, 1939), p. 42.
[9] Calder-Marshall, *op. cit.*, p. 221.
[10] "Inside the Empire", May 1940.
[11] "Declaration of Rights of the Caribbean Peoples to Self-Determination and Self-Government", 1940.
[12] L. Araquistain: *La Agonia Antillana* (Madrid, 1928), p. 70.

Chapter IX

[1] *The West Indies Today*, p. 30.

[2] *Restriction of Hours of Labour*, p. 12.

[3] *Labour Policy in Trinidad* ("International Labour Information", May 3, 1937), p. 184.

[4] *Franchise Commission.* Mr. Rapsey.

[5] *West India Royal Commission, 1938–39, Recommendations,* Cmd. 6174 (His Majesty's Stationery Office, 1940), p. 18.

[6] Cmd. 1679, p. 24.

[7] Quoted by G. Padmore: *"Democracy" for the West Indies* ("Crisis", June 1941), p. 189.

[8] "New York Times", July 16, 1941.

[9] *Foreign Trade of the United States, 1938* (U. S. Department of Commerce), pp. 48–49.

[10] M. M. Knight: *The Americans in Santo Domingo* (New York, 1928), p. 143.

[11] *Ibid.,* p. 176.

114

SELECT BIBLIOGRAPHY

This bibliography is not meant to be exhaustive. Its purpose is merely to indicate to the more serious reader some of the major and more useful sources for further information on the Caribbean, with special reference to the Negro, and with the emphasis less on political and diplomatic history than on social and economic conditions.

A. *Official Reports*

(a) British Islands:

Report of the West India Royal Commission, 1897.
Report of the Sugar Commission, 1929.
Report of the Trinidad Disturbances Commission, 1937.
Report of the Closer Union Commission, 1933.
Report of a Commission appointed to consider Problems of Secondary and Primary Education in Trinidad etc., 1931–32.
Report of a visit to certain West Indian colonies and to British Guiana (Major Wood), 1921.
Labour Conditions in the West Indies, 1937.
Recommendations of the West India Royal Commission, 1938–39.

These reports, by commissioners sent out from England, should be supplemented by the reports of various local commissions of which the most useful are:

Report on nutrition in the various colonies.
Report of the Barbados Disturbances Commission, 1937.
Report of Select Committee of the Legislative Council on Restriction of Hours of Labour, Trinidad, 1926.
Report of the British Guiana Franchise Commission, 1934.
Report of the Economic Investigation Committee, British Guiana, 1930.
Report of the Small Farmers Committee, British Guiana, 1930.
Commission of Inquiry into Labour Conditions, St. Lucia, 1937— Interim and Final Reports on the Sugar Industry.
Report by Minimum Wage Advisory Board in regard to . . . Agricultural Labourers, St. Lucia, 1936.
Report of a Commission to enquire into the Economic Condition of various classes of wage-earners in the Colony, Grenada, 1938.
Report on the Agricultural Conditions of Dominica, 1925.
Report of the Unemployment Commission, Jamaica, 1936.
Report of the Commissioners appointed to enquire into and report on the Labour Disputes . . . , British Guiana, 1935.
Report of the Labour Disturbances Commission, Trinidad, 1934.
Report of the Jamaica Banana Commission, 1936.

These reports, local and imperial, lay bare the conditions of the British West Indies; their number and their repetition of the same themes illustrate the inertia and indifference of governments not representative of the majority of the inhabitants.

(b) American Islands:
Annual Reports of the Governor, Department of Education, Commissioner of Labor in Puerto Rico.

Health and Socio-Economic Studies in Puerto Rico:
1. On a Sugar Cane Plantation.
2. In the Coffee, Fruit and Tobacco Regions.
3. Physical Measurements of Agricultural Workers.
4. Physical Impairments of Adult Life Among Agricultural Workers.
5. Health Work in the Rural Areas of Puerto Rico.
Five invaluable scientific studies.

E. A. Bird: Report on the Sugar Industry in Relation to the Social and Economic System of Puerto Rico, 1937.
Report of the Puerto Rico Policy Commission (Chardon Report), 1934.
E. W. Zimmermann: Staff Report to the Interdepartmental Committee on Puerto Rico, 1940.

These three reports represent official investigations of conditions in Puerto Rico. Their recommendations have been as usual ignored.

(c) Independent Islands:
Annual Reports of the American Fiscal Representative in Haiti and Dominican Republic.

B. Books
B. W. and J. W. Diffie: *Porto Rico, a Broken Pledge* (New York, 1931).
L. H. Jenks: *Our Cuban Colony* (New York, 1928).
M. M. Knight: *The Americans in Santo Domingo* (New York, 1928).

These three studies in American imperialism are of the greatest value today, as illustrating the inconsistency of dollar diplomacy with the policy of the good neighbor.

Foreign Policy Association: *Problems of the New Cuba* (New York, 1935). Full of useful information.
A. Calder-Marshall: *Glory Dead* (London, 1939). A sympathetic description of conditions in Trinidad and its people.
K. Pringle: *Waters of the West* (London, 1938). Includes a good chapter on Jamaica.
O. P. Starkey: *The Economic Geography of Barbados* (New York, 1939). A superficial book which does not live up to the pretentiousness of its title, but which includes some useful tables.
W. M. Macmillan: *Warning from the West Indies* (London, 1938). A good description by a South African Liberal professor, with conclusions typical of the academic liberal.
A Arredondo: *El Negro en Cuba* (La Habana, 1939). Useful for readers of Spanish.
The European Possessions in the Caribbean Area (American Geographical Society, 1941). A good compilation of facts and figures.

116

F. Ortiz: *Contrapunteo Cubano del Tabaco y el Azúcar* (La Habana, 1940). A brilliant analysis, by the greatest scholar of the Caribbean, on the respective roles of tobacco, a free white industry, and sugar, a black slave industry, in Cuban history, and the pernicious effects of foreign capitalism.

C. Pamphlets

The West Indies Today (published by the International African Service Bureau of London). Presents the case of progressive British colonials.

W. A. Lewis: *Labour in the West Indies* (London, 1939). An excellent short study by a West Indian student now a member of the Faculty of the London School of Economics.

R. Picó: *Studies in the Economic Geography of Puerto Rico* (Rio Piedras, 1937). A collection of three good studies by a member of the Faculty of the University of Puerto Rico.

E. B. Hill and S. L. Descartes: *An Economic Background for Agricultural Research in Puerto Rico* (Rio Piedras, 1939). Contains useful data.

C. L. R. James: *The Case for West Indian Self Government* (London, 1933). A British colonial's point of view.

M. Dartigue: *Conditions Rurales en Haiti* (Port-au-Prince, 1938). A very good analysis of Haitian agriculture.

Foreign Policy Reports (Foreign Policy Association, New York):

E. K. James: *Puerto Rico at the Crossroads,* Oct. 15, 1937.

L. H. Evans: *Unrest in the Virgin Islands,* March 27, 1935.

C. A. Thomson: *Dictatorship in the Dominican Republic,* April 15, 1936.

A. R. Elliott: *European Colonies in the Western Hemisphere,* August 15, 1940.

H. J. Trueblood: *The Havana Conference of 1940,* Sept. 15, 1940.

D. Articles

G. Simpson: *Haitian Peasant Economy* ("Journal of Negro History", October 1940). Excellent.

Price Mars: *Social Castes and Social Problems in Haiti* ("Inter-American Quarterly", July 1940). A discussion of Haitian society by Haiti's outstanding man of letters.

R. Picó: *Puerto Rico, Economic Sore Spot* ("Inter-American Quarterly", April 1940). A good article, by one of the foremost intellectual opponents of the large plantation.

W. A. Roberts: *Future of the British Caribbean* ("Survey Graphic", April 1941). A well-written and thoughtful article.

C. W. Taussig: *The Caribbean* ("Survey Graphic", March 1941). A superficial treatment by a writer apparently easily impressed by "paper" policies.

V. P. Tschebotareff: *New Problems for the British West Indies* ("Inter-American Quarterly", July 1941). Nothing new in the problems discussed.

Eric Williams: *The Negro in the British West Indies* (in "The Negro in the Americas", Graduate School, Howard University, 1940).

117

APPENDIX

The Caribbean Islands:—Area, Population and Trade.

Island	Area (Sq. miles)	Population	Exports (thousand dollars)	Percentage to U. S.	Imports (thousand dollars)	Percentage from U. S.
Independent						
Cuba.....................	44,000	(1940) 4,215,000	(1938) 142,678	75.9	106,007	70.9
Haiti...................	10,700	(1940) 2,700,000	(1940) 5,399	51.6	7,940	72.6
Dominican Republic........	19,332	(1937) 1,581,000	(1939) 18,643	27.1	11,592	59.2
American						
Puerto Rico..............	3,349	(1940) 1,869,200	(1939-40) 92,347	98.9	107,030	93.9
Virgin Islands.............	133	(1930) 22,000	(1939) 1,664	100	3,456	100
British						
Jamaica...................	4,450	(1938) 1,173,600	(1936) 18,342	7.	24,354	16.5
Trinidad & Tobago........	1,878	(1937) 456,000	29,944	13.	27,187	16.6
Barbados.................	166	(1938) 193,000	7,168	6.	9,621	10.4
Leeward Islands						
Antigua..................	108	(1938) 34,100	961	2.	1,001	16.5
St. Kitts-Nevis............	124	31,700	1,440	*	1,229	14.5
Montserrat...............	32	5,700	220	4.	298	11.2
Virgin Islands.............	67	6,300	52	82.5	51	19.
Windward Islands						
Dominica.................	305	(1938) 50,600	335	16.	590	10.
St. Lucia.................	233	69,000	891	13.	923	8.
St. Vincent...............	150	58,300	749	36.	839	13.
Grenada..................	133	88,200	1,375	26.	1,379	9.
Bahamas.................	4,375	67,720	682	26.	4,762	42.5
Bermuda.................	19	31,500	651	65.	9,080	38.4
French Islands						
Martinique...............	385	(1939) 241,000	(1938) 8,919	....	6,547	....
Guadeloupe...............	583	(1938) 304,200	(1937) 13,449	....	9,828	....
Dutch Islands						
Curaçao and smaller islands..	384	(1938) 101,000	(1937) 134,980	12.	148,651	13.
Mainland Territories						
British Guiana.............	90,000	(1938) 337,200	11,966	5.75	9,618	8.7
French Guiana.............	34,740	(1936) 42,600	(1937) 1,414	....	2,108	....
Dutch Guiana.............	50,000	(1939) 177,900	(1939) 3,981	71.8	3,943	30.
British Honduras..........	8,598	(1938) 57,700	2,413	36.	3,272	29.

* Indicates less than one per cent.

The table does not include smaller islands like the Turks and Caicos Islands (5,300 population) and Cayman Islands (6,000)— both dependencies of Jamaica; the Isle of Pines, off Cuba; Vieques

(51 sq. mi., 10,000 population), off Puerto Rico; Marie-Galante (58 sq. mi.), Desirade (14.5 sq. mi.), Petite-Terre (1.5 sq. mi.), Les Saintes (5.5 sq. mi.), St. Bartholomew (8.3 sq. mi.), the French part of St. Martin (20 sq. mi.)—all dependencies of Guadeloupe. The figures for Curaçao (170 sq. mi.), Aruba (70 sq. mi.), Bonaire (108 sq. mi.), St. Eustatius (12 sq. mi.), Saba (5 sq. mi.), and the Dutch part of St. Martin (13 sq. mi.) are combined.

The statistics come from the following sources:

(a) Independent islands: *The Foreign Trade of Latin America, Part II* (U. S. Tariff Commission, Washington, 1940).

(b) American islands: *Annual Book on Statistics* (Puerto Rico, 1939–1940); *Annual Report of the Governor of the Virgin Islands, 1940; The Virgin Islands of the United States* (Washington, 1939).

(c) British islands: *Report on the Economic and Commercial Conditions in the British West Indies* (London, 1937); *The European Possessions in the Caribbean Area* (American Geographical Society, 1941). British trade figures are for the year 1936, changed into dollars at the rate of £1 = $4.80.

(d) Dutch islands: *The European Possessions in the Caribbean Area.* The Dutch guilder has been transferred to American currency at the 1937 rate of 1 guilder = 55 cents.

(e) French islands: *The European Possessions in the Caribbean Area.* The rate of exchange in 1937 was 1 franc = 4 cents.

The table calls for some explanation:

(a) For the area as a whole the United States sells more than she buys.

(b) The high percentage of exports from the British Virgin Islands is probably to be explained by some confusion with the American Virgin Islands.

(c) The large imports from the United States into the Bahamas and Bermuda are to be attributed to their large tourist trade with the mainland as well as to their proximity. This tourist trade brought the Bahamas about five million dollars in 1936.

(d) French colonial trade is dominated by France. Assuming that the trade of Martinique in 1937 was equal to the figures for 1938 (strictly incorrect, because of the rise of the franc from two to four cents), total French colonial exports for 1937 were 23,782 and imports 18,483 (thousand dollars). United States purchases from the "French West Indies" in 1937 were 233, and exports 2,247 (thousand dollars), one per cent and twelve per cent respectively of the islands' figures (Foreign Trade of the United States, 1938). This confirms the general statement above, that the United States sells more than she buys.

(e) Where United States imports are high, as in Dutch Guiana, those imports are not in sugar or tropical produce (Cuba, Puerto Rico and the Virgin Islands excepted) but in bauxite (hence the recent despatch of United States troops to that area).

(f) The comparatively large trade figures for the Dutch island possessions are explained by the vast imports and exports of oil. The oil of Venezuela and Colombia, due to poor harbor facilities in those places, is piped into Curaçao and Aruba, where some of the world's largest refineries are located. Economically, the Dutch islands are a part of those two mainland areas rather than the Caribbean proper.

EWorld Inc.
Send for our complete full color catalog today!

A BOOK OF THE BEGINNINGS VOL. I & II (SET)	*MASSEY*	49.95
AFRIKAN HOLISTIC HEALTH	*AFRIKA*	19.95
AFRICAN DISCOVERY OF AMERICA	*WEINER*	15.95
ANACALYPSIS (SET)	*MASSEY*	49.95
ARAB INVASION OF EGYPT		16.95
ANKH: AFRICAN ORIGIN OF ELECTROMAGNETISM		10.95
AIDS THE END OF CIVILIZATION	*DOUGLASS*	9.95
BABY NAMES:REAL NAMES WITH REAL MEANINGS FOR AFRICAN CHILDREN		12.95
BLACK HEROES OF THE MARTIAL ARTS	*VAN CLIEF*	16.95
APOCRYPHA (HC)		14.95
BRITISH HISTORIANS & THE WEST INDIES	*ERIC WILLIAMS*	14.95
CHRISTOPHER COLUMBUS & THE AFRICAN HOLOCAUST	*JOHN HENRIK CLARKE*	10.95
COLUMBUS CONSPIRACY	*BRADLEY*	14.95
DAWN VOYAGE:THE BLACK AFRICAN DISCOVERY OF AMERICA	*BRADLEY*	14.95
DOCUMENTS OF WEST INDIAN HISTORY	*ERIC WILLIAMS*	15.95
EDUCATION OF THE NEGRO	*CARTER G. WOODSON*	14.95
EGYPTIAN BOOK OF THE DEAD	*BUDGE*	16.95
EGYPTIAN BOOK OF THE DEAD/ANCIENT MYSTERIES OF AMENTA	*MASSEY*	9.95
FIRST COUNCIL OF NICE: A WORLD'S CHRISTIAN CONVENTION A.D. 325		10.95
FORBIDDEN BOOKS OF THE NEW TESTAMENT		14.95
GERALD MASSEY'S LECTURES		10.95
GLOBAL AFRIKAN PRESENCE	*EDWARD SCOBIE*	15.95
GOSPEL OF BARNABAS		14.95
GREATER KEY OF SOLOMON		10.00
HAIRLOCKING: EVERYTHING YOU NEED TO KNOW	*NEKHENA EVANS*	9.95
HARLEM VOICES FROM THE SOUL OF BLACK AMERICA	*JOHN HENRIK CLARKE*	10.95
HARLEM USA	*JOHN HENRIK CLARKE*	10.95
HEAL THYSELF FOR HEALTH AND LONGEVITY	*QUEEN AFUA*	18.95
HEAL THYSELF COOKBOOK:HOLISTIC COOKING WITH JUICES	*DIANE CICCONE*	13.95
HISTORICAL JESUS & THE MYTHICAL CHRIST	*GERALD MASSEY*	9.95
HISTORY OF THE PEOPLE OF TRINIDAD & TOBAGO	*ERIC WILLIAMS*	15.95
LOST BOOKS OF THE BIBLE & THE FORGOTTEN BOOKS OF EDEN		14.95
NUTRITION MADE SIMPLE; AT A GLANCE		8.95
SIGNS & SYMBOLS OF PRIMORDIAL MAN		17.95
VITAMINS & MINERALS A TO Z	*JEWEL POOKRUM*	13.95
WHAT THEY NEVER TOLD YOU IN HISTORY CLASS VOL. ONE	*CUSH*	19.95
FREEMASONRY INTERPRETED		12.95
FREEMASONRY & THE VATICAN		11.95
FREEMASONRY & JUDAISM		11.95
FREEMASONRY:CHARACTER CLAIMS		13.95
FREEMASONRY EXPOSITION: EXPOSITION & ILLUSTRATIONS OF FREEMASONRY		9.95
SCIENCE OF MELANIN		14.95
SECRET SOCIETIES & SUBVERSIVE MOVEMENTS		13.95

Prices subject to change without notice

Mail To: EWorld Inc. - 1609 Main St. - Buffalo - New York - 14209
TEL: (716) 882-1704 FAX: (716)882-1708 EMAIL: eeworldinc@yahoo.com

NAME _____

ADDRESS _____

CITY _____ ST _____ ZIP _____